Santa Claus

COLLECTION

"A much greater joy comes from learning to tap into and appreciate the beauty that is already around you."

Bradley Bruinsma

Santa Claus

COLLECTION

Volume 4

Better Homes and Gardens® Creative Collection™
Des Moines, Iowa

Photograph by Perry Struse

Opposite: This "Mountain Santa on a Log" is just one of the delightful characters given life by sculptor and doll maker Anne Chase Sanregret. Meet the rest of her charming cast of Santas on pages 102–109.

The Spirit Lives On...

The night before Christmas isn't the longest night of the year just because of the winter solstice. As any child will tell you—or as you might even recall—a night spent waiting for the arrival of Santa Claus is a night that seems to go on forever.

With this fourth volume of the *Santa Claus Collection*, we've tried to recapture those feelings of childlike anticipation and wonder. It wasn't all that difficult. The spirit of Santa Claus resonates through the work of each of the painters, sculptors, carvers, and artisans whose masterpieces you're about to see. It's in the hearts of "Sgt. Santa" and "Father Christmas," two men who've adopted the jolly old man's persona and now bring the miracle of the season with them wherever they go. And it's implicit in the history and lore of the man we call St. Nick, a history our writers lovingly retell.

But to truly appreciate the spirit of Santa Claus, you'll want to add your own special contribution to the legacy. That's easy, too, with the creative projects and recipes you'll find here. Whether it's with a cross-stitch tree ornament or a batch of decorated cookies, you'll find lots of opportunities to express your own sentiments.

It's our sincere hope that, with every turn of the page, this volume of the *Santa Claus Collection* will delight you, inspire you, and make you feel like a kid again.

Believe!

Table of
Contents

Opposite: *Typical of the fine detail for which D. Blümchen & Company is known, the glitter on this poured papier-mâché candy container is applied by hand. Read more about the company on* pages 34–39.

Photograph by Perry Struse

LASTING LEGENDS

Jolly old St. Nick
actually is but one of a long line
of famous gift bringers
whose legacy lives on
to this day.

This cartoon showing children spying on Santa Claus as he prepares to descend the chimney is an undated work by Thomas Nast, whose nineteenth-century depictions of Santa captured America's heart.

A Man on a Mission

THE RESIDENTS OF RICHMOND, VIRGINIA, NEVER TIRE OF
SALUTING SERGEANT SANTA FOR HIS QUARTER-CENTURY-PLUS
OF SPREADING LOVE AND CHARITY.

Opposite: *Few would contend that Sergeant Ricky Duling needs much in the way of makeup to assume his role as Sgt. Santa each Christmas. "I figure God made me look this way and gave me this gift," he humbly says.*

It's amazing how we can open up a world of new possibilities with one simple life choice. Take Sergeant Ricky Duling. When this tough undercover police officer innocently adopted the persona of "Sgt. Santa" at a Christmas charity event in 1972, his life was forever changed.

"Let's put it this way," he says. "I used to have plenty of room when I'd walk down the sidewalk. Everyone would get out of my way!" Now he's an instantly recognizable personality—a man on a mission to see that no Richmond-area child goes without a Christmas. Along with his legendary gift-giving efforts during the holidays, he's also known for his year-round help to needy families. As Sgt. Santa, he has donated his time and talents to help thousands of people. And to think it all started with bubble gum.

"Back in the 1950s, parents sometimes used police officers to help discipline their kids, so they were scared to death of us," Duling explains. "I started throwing them gum from my squad car to help them overcome their fear." Gradually the kids began to trust him.

Written by Barbara Folkerts ◆ Photographs by Randy Foulds

AN UNLIKELY SANTA

With thirty-five years on the police force, many of them as sergeant, and several family members who wear the badge, Duling has law enforcement in his blood. He also has worked in intelligence and has provided security for everyone from Elvis Presley and other rock stars to Martin Luther King Jr. and U.S. presidents. Hardly the kind of fellow you'd picture in a Santa suit!

But in 1972 he was asked to play Santa in a sporting-goods store commercial, simply because he looked the part. He balked at the proposal at first but finally accepted—only after the store agreed to donate hundreds of dollars' worth of equipment to the police camp for deserving children where he helped out each summer.

"The good Lord started working against me at that point!" Duling jokes. Wishing he could reach out more to the area's underprivileged children, he came up with an idea. If he wore his Santa suit into the projects on Christmas Eve, he could pass out presents, possibly even from his police cruiser. And with the department's okay, that's just what he did. That first year, with lights flashing and siren blaring, he gave out three hundred boxes of candy. One boy recognized him as Sergeant Duling from summer camp and yelled, "It's Sgt. Santa!"

THE REST IS HISTORY

Now, nearly thirty years later, thousands of volunteers from Boy Scouts to civic groups help Sgt. Santa prepare for the big event. Some businesses even close early so their employees can take part. Together, they assemble a multitude of gift packages, each containing a comic book, crayons, cookies, candy, and a small toy. "We don't recruit volunteers," Duling explains. "They ask if they can help. It's amazing."

For nearly eighteen hours on Christmas Eve, Sgt. Santa delivers gifts nonstop, not even stopping for meals. While he empties one carload, a second car is stocked and waiting. Then on Christmas morning, he takes orphaned boys from the Virginia Home for

Boys to the police lodge, where they're treated to a big breakfast and special gifts.

This annual tradition really exploded in 1989 when Duling officially retired and became Sgt. Santa full-time in conjunction with Richmond's Bureau of Police. As of Christmas 2001, the number of gifts had multiplied to more than 17,500, each one still personally delivered. And that's just for starters.

In addition, Sgt. Santa has established a year-round nonprofit organization that provides food, clothing, and furniture to people in need of assistance, all free of charge. Patrons simply come to "Sgt. Santa's Workshop," a warehouse operated solely by volunteers, and pick out whatever they need. The organization has helped more than thirteen hundred families at Christmas and countless others throughout the year.

Opposite: On the day before Christmas, Sgt. Santa works nonstop personally delivering thousands of gift packages to Richmond-area children. The packages are lovingly assembled by his legion of faithful volunteer "elves."

Above: The legend of Sgt. Santa was born innocently enough. As a way of reaching out to the city's underprivileged kids, on Christmas Eve 1972 Sergeant Duling donned a Santa suit and cruised the housing projects in his police car passing out boxes of candy.

One of Sgt. Santa's most rewarding—and most touching—duties is lending a friendly ear to the hopes and dreams of the eager children who seek him out.

Opposite: "Sgt. Santa's Workshop" is a volunteer-staffed warehouse that operates year-round to provide food, clothing, and furniture to those in need. It's also where toys are stockpiled for Sgt. Santa's Christmas Eve rounds.

"If there ever comes a time when I have to solicit money, I'll know it's time to stop," Duling says. "I could never do this work by myself. It's the good Lord who makes it happen."

When he's not at the warehouse, Sgt. Santa is visiting hospitals or doing other charitable deeds, all in full costume. To say that he squeezes more into a day at seventy-four years old than many do at half his age is an understatement. His wife, Dale, used to accompany him as the "Snow Queen" but gave it up because, she says, he moved too fast!

"Someone once told me I must be a robot to keep a schedule like this," he says. "Some days in December, I work until 3 or 4 a.m. and then speak at a breakfast meeting at 6:30. But the Lord gives me the strength to get through each day."

"THEY KEEP US CRYING"

Perhaps the hardest part of the job is hearing the countless sad stories that children tell "Santa." One time a preschool-age boy told him, "My mommy died in August. When you go back in the sky, would you please tell her I love her and I'm doing okay?" On another occasion an underprivileged five-year-old gave him a nickel and two pennies, saying, "Santa, please use this to help some little poor child."

And there was the Russian family who knew no English and had no resources. When Sgt. Santa was able to provide them with furniture and even bicycles for their children, the father cried, explaining they could never afford bikes in Russia. With no other way to thank him, the man insisted that Sgt. Santa accept the military medals he had earned as a captain. "They keep us crying," Duling says.

Although the hours are long and the pay is measured only in human gratitude, Sgt. Santa finds great joy and satisfaction in his work. "I figure God made me look this way and gave me this gift. It's the greatest thing that's ever happened to me. Every day I make a lot of people happy, and that makes it all worthwhile."✦

A Midwest Father Christmas

THIS MERRY WANDERER SPREADS AUTHENTIC OLD-WORLD HOLIDAY CHEER IN THE HEARTLAND.

Opposite: *Together with a carefully attired troupe of period characters, Alan Lance Andersen has built a loyal following in towns throughout Iowa and Illinois with his elaborately staged appearances as Father Christmas.*

Among all the flying scarves, clomping boots, and swirling snow, children run toward Father Christmas. They crane their necks and look up. And up, and up. Father Christmas is a towering giant, standing six feet six inches tall in his Christmas stockings. With his fur-trimmed hat and boots, he's nearly seven feet tall. Weighing in at over four hundred pounds and sporting a sixty-inch waist, he naturally commands attention.

Father Christmas beams at the children, many of whom already have e-mailed him and checked out his Web site. The kids pop rapid-fire questions:

"Are you Santa Claus?"

"No, but I'm Santa's great-great-great-grandfather. They say there's a family resemblance, don't you think?" he asks as he strokes his flowing white beard.

"Do you live in the North Pole?"

"No, I live in the Black Forest," he explains. "The Black Forest is an enchanted realm that exists in many

Written by Marie McCartan ✦ *Photographs by Craig Anderson*

places at the same time. There is a Black Forest in
Germany, in Austria, and in Switzerland. A tiny little
sliver of its magic is even found along the greenbelt
between Story City and Ames right here in Iowa."

Father Christmas then explains that his family dates
all the way back to St. Nicholas in the fourth century.
"While Santa brings gifts to children around the world,
I preside over the wassail bowl and yule log. I take
orders for presents, and Santa does the deliveries. The
last time I tried to climb down a chimney, I got stuck!"
says Father Christmas with a grin and a pat of his
gigantic tummy.

Amazingly nimble for his size, Father Christmas
often dances in the street. He's even been known to
pluck a grandmother from the crowd to be his dance
partner while cavorting to the music of a tuba player
or bagpipes. He also likes to give the Salvation Army
bell ringers a hand, and he's a big-time hugger. "I open
my arms wide, and if people want a hug they'll come
forward," he explains. "And it's not just children who
like hugs," Father Christmas says. "I'm always surprised
at the adults who want—or need—a hug, too."

THE REAL FATHER CHRISTMAS

Who exactly is this centuries-old legend seemingly
come to life? He's Alan Lance Andersen, director of
the Theatre of Interactive Drama in Roland, Iowa, a
bucolic community of just over one thousand people.
It's from Roland that Alan researches the legends and
lore of Father Christmas and assumes the elaborate
persona he uses to spread his holiday goodwill.

Together with a carefully attired troupe of period
characters he calls his "retinue," Alan has built a loyal
following in towns throughout Iowa and Illinois with
his carefully staged appearances as Father Christmas.
Sometimes his supporting cast of minstrels and actors
will appear in Victorian finery; other venues may
demand Renaissance garb. But whatever costumes they
don, this merry band can include everything from
nineteenth-century carolers, jugglers, and wandering
puppeteers to Raggedy Ann and characters from the
stories of Charles Dickens and Mother Goose.

As for Father Christmas himself, Alan prefers more
eclectic attire. He carries a handmade leather drinking
mug on his belt, packs hand-carved wooden toys in
his deerskin pouch, and moves with a walking staff
decorated with elaborate Norwegian rosemaling, gold
and silver bells, and pinecones.

Most of Father Christmas's appearances take place
at outdoor venues, and the Midwest is known for its
harsh winters. But thanks to his elaborate costume,
Alan shrugs off the weather. His usual wardrobe
includes a heavy red and burgundy tunic, complete
with rich brocade and gold embroidery. It's all topped
off with a mantled green greatcoat that's trimmed with
three full sheepskins. It's not unusual to hear Father
Christmas proclaim, "The colder, the better!"

Father Christmas is known to give out hugs to people in the crowd. "I open my arms wide, and if people want a hug they'll come forward," he says. "And it's not just children who like hugs."

Below: It's not unusual for Father Christmas to entertain a crowd with everything from medieval ballads to obscure tales of Christmas lore from foreign lands.

AN AMBASSADOR OF GOODWILL

Legend has it that Father Christmas and Santa Claus (as well as St. Nicholas) are related to a host of other famous holiday personages with global ties, including Grandfather Frost and Tatiana the Snow Princess (in Russia) and Zinter Klaus (in Holland). So it's only natural for Alan to entertain holiday crowds with everything from medieval ballads to tales of Christmas lore from around the world.

In keeping with Father Christmas's international heritage, Alan proudly delivers holiday greetings in more than twenty languages. There's "Snovum Godum," which means "Happy Snow" in Russian; "Joyeux Noël," or "Joyful Christmas," in French; "Feliz Navidad" in Spanish; "Heilige Weihnachten" in German; and "Glædelig Jul" in Danish, to mention just a few. And for Jewish festivalgoers, he offers, "Happy Hanukkah."

Alan never knows when these greetings are going to come in handy. One holiday when he was appearing as Father Christmas in Muscatine, Iowa, his host introduced him to "a family visiting from Georgia." Noting their dark eyes and black hair, he said, "Ah, these people are not from the state of Georgia—they are from the country of Georgia."

Clapping her hands together in wonder, the woman exclaimed, "Oh, he knows our country!" And when Father Christmas took her hand and intoned "Snovum Godum" complete with heavy accent, her eyes went wide. They all began speaking excitedly in Russian

and went away shaking their heads in wonder and saying, "It's true—he really does speak all languages!"

That's but one example of why this Father Christmas says he has the best job in the world. "I see lots of smiles. I get lots of hugs. I get to feel the magic of Christmas every day of the season."✦

This portrait of Father Christmas shows why the "old, hearty, and wise" gent was so popular in England during the late Middle Ages.

What child hasn't dreamt of a rooftop Santa like this one, whose cautionary gesture warns to make nary a sound lest the sleepers below awaken.

The Gift Bringers

ALTHOUGH GIFT GIVING IS NO DOUBT SANTA'S CLAIM TO FAME,
HE DOESN'T WORK ALONE. HE SHARES HIS PHILANTHROPIC SPIRIT
WITH GIFT BRINGERS THE WORLD OVER.

With the story of the Magi, or Three Wise Men, who brought precious gifts to Baby Jesus, the idea of gift bearing seems unalterably linked with Christmas. The legends of the Magi and their travels inspired stories of other gift bringers whose stories remain enlightening.

Some gift bringers have their origins in pagan times, like Berchta, the winter goddess of northern Europe. Tending to home and hearth, this guardian of children and protector of the fields was reputed to fly through the skies during the Twelve Days of Christmas.

In Scandinavia, mischievous Christmas gnomes, or Jultomten, came out from their hiding places under stairs and in attics to distribute gifts and raise occasional havoc. Believing that these elves guarded the household, people offered porridge and milk to appease them.

Russian legend tells of children receiving gifts from an old woman, or Babushka, who they believed delivered trinkets every Epiphany (January 6). As the story goes, Babushka had been visited by the Magi in search of the King but turned them away to tend to her chores. Later regretting her decision, she roamed the earth in an endless search for the Christ Child, leaving gifts en route for well-behaved children. Italy tells a similar story of a witchlike figure named La Befana, also known as La Strega (the witch) or La Vecchia (the old woman).

England's late-Middle Ages Father Christmas originally did not distribute gifts but simply personified the joy of the season. A central figure in early mummers' plays (a form of folk merrymaking and entertainment), Father Christmas was old, hearty, and wise. The Germans call him Weihnachtsmann. The French call him Père Noël, a solemn old man in a long hooded robe with white fur trim who possessed a gentle spirit. Influenced by the growing popularity of America's Santa Claus, Father Christmas has since assumed a new identity, more like Santa than his original folk image.

Written by Judith Stern Friedman
All artwork courtesy of Bettmann/CORBIS

SETTING THE STANDARD

Perhaps the most widely known gift bringer of legend is Santa's predecessor, from the Dutch Sinter Klaas or St. Nicholas. A hero of the third and fourth centuries A.D., Nicholas was born in the village of Patara on the Mediterranean Sea (now part of Turkey). A young and passionate Bishop of Myra, he was imprisoned for his faith under the Roman Empire but held fast to Christianity and converted many believers.

Throughout his life, Nicholas was revered for his wisdom and generosity. One famous legend tells how he saved a penniless Myra father who contemplated selling his three daughters into slavery. When Nicholas heard of the old man's plight, he waited until dark and then threw bags of gold through an opening in the wall. (In another variation, he threw the gold through a window.) The bags landed in stockings the girls had hung near the fire to dry, and they found them there with surprise and delight the next morning.

Other legends of saving sailors, protecting children, and promoting goodwill earned Nicholas sainthood shortly after his death on December 6, 343. By the Renaissance, he was Europe's most popular saint. Hundreds of churches were built in his name, people enacted plays to tell his stories, and St. Nicholas Day was heralded as a time of celebration.

St. Nicholas Day is still recognized today in the Netherlands, the Czech Republic, Slovakia, Austria, and other European countries. On December 5, children set out shoes and stockings by the fireplace or window in hopes of receiving gifts from St. Nicholas just like the maidens of Myra.

Although people continued to celebrate St. Nicholas Day and the magical flights of spirits on Epiphany, the Protestant Reformation moved the celebration to December 24, in the sixteenth century. Religious leaders communicated the importance of receiving gifts directly from God, rather than from saints, witches, or elves. Christkindel, or the Christ Child, was the angel-like deliverer who traveled house to house on a donkey. (Later in America, the Christkindel lore eventually faded, and the name evolved into the familiar Kris Kringle, now associated with Santa Claus.

COMMON GROUND

Over the years, the legend of the gift bringers has evolved with cultural, religious, and historic events. With the rise of Communism (1917–1991), for instance, Babushka and St. Nicholas were replaced with the secular Grandfather Frost, who delivers gifts on New Year's Eve accompanied by his granddaughter, Snegurochka (the Snow Maiden).

Although all of these gift bringers are good at heart, many are said to have a sinister counterpart, typically portrayed as an old, dark character who bears threatening consequences for wayward children. Most carry a switch and follow along in the gift bringer's shadow. St. Nicholas's sidekick, Black Peter, appears in several forms: Zwarte Piet in the Netherlands, Cert in Czechoslovakia, Père Fouettard ("Father Whip") in France, and in Germany, Pelz Nicholas ("Fur Nicholas") who eventually became Belsnickle when the Pennsylvania Dutch brought him to America.

In every case, however, good prevails over bad, and people find comfort in their benevolent heroes. Whatever form these gift bringers take, they deliver much more than the gifts in their sacks. Their colorful stories, positive examples, and lively traditions bring families together and help renew our holiday spirit.◆

St. Nicholas was one of the most fabled gift bringers of all. As the Bishop of Myra, he was imprisoned for his beliefs yet held fast to his faith and won many converts.

TIMELESS MEMORABILIA

A reverence for days gone by
is the common thread that unites
the artists you'll meet here.
Thanks to their creativity and
dedication, we all can revel in the
wonders of Christmas Past.

*How sweet it is! This ornate Father Christmas
was cast from an antique chocolate mold originally
designed for a German confectionery shop. (From the
collection of Judi and Gary Vaillancourt)*

Photograph by Perry Struse

Sweet (Santa) Success

BY GIVING HER PAINTED OLD WORLD SANTAS A SECOND LIFE, ARTIST JUDI VAILLANCOURT KEEPS A SLICE OF CHRISTMAS HISTORY ALIVE.

Opposite: *In the Vaillancourt retail store, a selection of Old World Santa figures and ornaments presents an enticing window display.*

Here is the measure of how determined the collectors of Vaillancourt Folk Art's Starlight Series Santas can be. Early each November, Judi and Gary Vaillancourt unveil their company's newest chalkware ornament that benefits the Starlight Children's Foundation, an organization that assists chronically and terminally ill children. The unveiling takes place at the company's studio and gallery in an old colonial farmhouse in Sutton, Massachusetts.

A day and a half before each unveiling, about two dozen avid collectors set up camp in the studio driveway. They hunker down in campers or pitch tents. There's a friendly competition to be at the front of the line and snag an ornament with a low edition number, but despite the jockeying for position, a party atmosphere prevails. Gary builds a fire in the outdoor fireplace and dispenses libations and hot breakfasts to the faithful.

Written by Allison Engel ✦ Photographs by Perry Struse

The first buyers in the store get to take their pick of the chalkware figures and often take up to half an hour choosing the facial expressions that most appeal to them. Only then does Judi number the ornaments, awarding the first person in line the coveted number one. The Starlight Series Santa ornaments are sold only through Christmas Eve and have proven to be highly collectible.

BREAKING THE MOLD

The objects of this fervent attention are painted fine-chalkware figurines made from antique chocolate molds. Judi began collecting the molds nearly twenty years ago and now owns more than three thousand of them, including molds for hard barley candy and ice cream. Many of her molds are Old World Santa figures from Europe, with an emphasis on those made by master molder Anton Reiche of Dresden, Germany. A vintage catalog for Reiche's company listed a staggering three thousand different molds for Belsnickles, or "Nicholas in fur" figures. Judi knows this because she owns two of his original catalogs—part of the exhaustive library she uses to research each piece she produces.

In the 1800s, she notes, every small European village had a fine chocolate shop, and each produced dozens of molded chocolate Father Christmases, angels, and Easter animals. During World War II, however, many molds were melted down for scrap. In the 1960s, a shift to acrylic molds made metal molds virtually obsolete. They ended up in antique stores, which is where Gary

Vaillancourt found his first three acquisitions back in 1984. He gave them to Judi innocently enough, never dreaming that his gift would change their lives.

Judi, a fine arts major in college, had been a painter and designer of historic furniture and mantels. Always having admired folk art, she saw the molds as an inspired source of painted ornaments. She first began molding ornaments from beeswax but soon found that they took too long to harden. She then switched to chalkware and later graduated to fine-grained plaster of the quality used in dental work and porcelain fixtures. "It's a smooth, velvety surface that absorbs paint beautifully," she says. "Painting each figure is like creating a small canvas."

So even though the medium isn't really chalk, the chalkware name persists. Today, chalkware painting is subtle and refined, but when it began in 1840s Italy, it was with garish, unrealistic designs meant as decorative accents for mantels. Painters would create green squirrels with yellow polka dots, for example, or deer figurines in bizarre colors. These early chalkware examples now are eagerly sought out.

A BUSINESS IS BORN

Not long after she received those first chocolate molds, Judi displayed one of her first chalkware pieces at a local art show and received orders for thirty more. A business was born, growing so rapidly that two years later, Gary, who was in the corporate world of sales and computers, joined the company full-time.

Above: *Judi and Gary Vaillancourt are shown with Christmas dinnerware that Judi designed and had made in England. The pattern is called Classical Christmas.*

Opposite: *"Civil War Santa," first produced in 1990, is one of the company's most popular figures. It appeals to those looking for a patriotic piece.*

Today, her figurines are sold in gift shops, Christmas stores, and department stores nationwide as well as in thirty-seven exclusive stores from coast to coast that have been deemed her "master dealers." An active secondary market also exists for limited-edition pieces retired by the company. Judi now makes all the samples and does one-of-a-kind custom work. In their historic 1840s studio, more than a dozen artists pour molds and laboriously apply oil paints to the tiny figurines. The company's inventory includes more than one thousand figures, more than half of them Christmas-related.

"In Europe, Christmas lasts for two weeks. But in this country, it now goes on for two months," Judi says. "I think it's a nostalgic longing for better days that has made Christmas so big. It's that moment of sanity in our lives that we cling to. Christmas is the time of year when people are extranice. It just changes everyone. In that respect, I'd like to see it last even longer!"

In 1997, the couple decided to start a line of glass Christmas ornaments based on their chalkware designs. Searching for high-quality glass production, they chose artisans in the old German town of Lauscha to make their glass ornaments. It was there that the four hundredth anniversary of glassblowing was celebrated several years ago. Lauscha also is the town where F. W. Woolworth himself traveled in 1889 to purchase blown-glass figural ornaments—which he introduced to America—to sell in his stores.

All of the Vaillancourt Folk Art glass ornaments are replicas of its chalkware figurines. The glass ornaments are painted with an unglazed finish, which matches the matte finish of the chalkware. Every year, the company also creates a limited-edition glass ornament as a companion piece to its Starlight figurine. The 2001 Starlight ornament was an angel pushing a long, flat, empty sleigh, with Father Christmas out front pulling.

Dutch St. Nicholas figures from the early nineteenth century always rode on white horses.

THE HOMEWORK NEVER ENDS

Judi carefully studies Christmas history and buys any book on Christmas traditions and customs she can find. In a converted barn that's part of the couple's 1690 saltbox home, there's an entire room lined with bookshelves. Her shelves hold Christmas books, and Gary's hold volumes on the Civil War and science fiction.

From her research, Judi can discern geographic differences in the Father Christmas images. For example, the placement of the arms or whether the figure carries a switch or a sack can pinpoint the origin of an Old World Santa. Even looking at what's inside the sack can be instructive, she says. The earliest molds showed St. Nicholas carrying only apples and oranges, the latter of which would have been considered an extravagant gift at the time. Toys did not appear until much later.

"So many of the Christmas images in this country were set by Thomas Nast or illustrated ads for Coca-Cola," Judi says. "We don't see Old World Father Christmases as much, and that's why these vintage molds represent an important glimpse into the past."

Using them "is an excuse to give these old molds a folklore," the artist continues. "They are important snapshots into Christmas. By depicting them, we're saving them. We're giving them another shot at life."✦

Top Left: *Linda Hettle, the manager of the pouring department at Vaillancourt Folk Art, pours chalkware.* Top Right: This *detail of a paint palette in the Vaillancourt studio is practically a work of art all by itself.* Bottom Left: *Francis Vaillancourt, 75, Gary's father, has worked for his son's company since he retired twenty years ago. Here, he trims the edges of a figure after it's been taken from a mold.* Bottom Right: *One of the company's most elaborate pieces is a Santa on a large sleigh. It takes forty hours to paint and sells for $1,500.*

Reviving an Old World Tradition

LOOSELY TRANSLATED, THE GERMAN WORD "BLÜMCHEN" MEANS
"LITTLE FLOWERS." THAT D. BLÜMCHEN & COMPANY'S OFFERINGS HAVE
BLOSSOMED INTO A FULL-BLOWN BOUQUET OF EUROPEAN-STYLE
CHRISTMAS COLLECTIBLES SEEMS MORE THAN APPROPRIATE.

*Opposite: Accessories for Blümchen's
original Santas may range from
authentic miniature German pewter
horns to handmade cornucopias.*

*Above: Some of Blümchen's "scraps"
originated in nineteenth-century Germany,
and were obtained when Berlin companies
closed in the late 1980s.*

Christmas in the Boyce household has always been truly a season, not just a day. With the onset of Advent four weeks before Christmas, this New Jersey family celebrates through the church calendar's Epiphany (January 6) in a home lavishly decorated with lovely antique ornaments.

As daughters Deborah and Diane became adults, they inherited their mother Beatrice's love for Old World Christmas ornaments. By the early 1980s, though, it was becoming more difficult to find such pieces on their New York City shopping trips. As other collectors caught on to their scarcity, garage sales and antique shops soon dried up as sources for the elaborately crafted European ornaments.

Written by Debra Gibson   ✦   Photographs by Perry Struse

For the three Boyce women, there seemed to be only one solution to the decorations dilemma—and D. Blümchen & Company, Inc., was born in 1985. Mom Beatrice handles marketing and public relations, while Deborah manages the day-to-day operations. Diane, a graduate of the Rhode Island School of Design, heads up the creative efforts. Nearly twenty years after the launch of the business, she laughs at her family's naïveté in launching their endeavor.

OFF AND RUNNING

"We were like the Little Rascals: 'Hey, let's put on a play!'" Diane remembers. "We chipped in some money, came up with a name, and went to our first trade show in New York. The few old-style ornaments that were there were of no quality. So then we went to the New York Gift Fair—they weren't there, either. We took books and pictures with us to the Nuremberg [Germany] Toy Fair, but forget it. Their antique-style ornaments now had plastic and sparkles on them."

It was clear: If they wanted traditional Christmas ornaments, they would have to produce them themselves. Armed with ornaments from their own personal collections, the Boyces returned to Germany and began knocking on the doors of ornament manufacturers. They were convinced that the companies still owned the original molds for these keepsakes; they just had to persuade the creators to go back to their roots and produce them once more. Their initial efforts were rebuffed, time and again.

So they went back to the drawing board—literally. The women crafted their own prototypes, returned to the European factories, and, in a stroke of genius, implied that the samples had been made by competitors. At last, deals were struck.

Today the company's inventory boasts both vintage European ornaments and original creations. Diane designs all new products, and about 25 percent of those are handcrafted by the seven staff artists working in the Ridgewood, New Jersey, company headquarters—a wonderful old building that dates back to 1789. The rest are created mostly by German artists, lthough some work also is done by artisans in the Czech Republic and Poland. Regardless of their origin, all the pieces truly reflect the company's goal of offering "The Best of Christmas Past®."

Above: *Mother-daughter professional partners for nearly twenty years, Beatrice and Diane Boyce began collaborating on home art projects when Diane was just a child.*

One small Blümchen ornament can require twenty to forty components.

Blümchen artists pride themselves on creating
traditional-style ornaments that feature
antique trims and quality craftsmanship.

"We try to create items with personalities,"
Diane Boyce says. "Blümchen is our therapy."

WELCOME BACK TO THE PAST

For many collectors, perusing the company's annual catalog is almost as gratifying as unwrapping a Christmas gift. The beautifully photographed 44-page wish book illustrates the wide variety of old-fashioned decorations, from Lithuanian candle houses to Victorian Whimseys® to Nativity scenes. But it may be the eclectic collection of Santas that sparks the most interest.

Take, for instance, the company's old-fashioned candy containers. Inspired by early-twentieth-century antiques, these Santas are crafted with papier-mâché heads, custom-made hands and boots created in Germany, and handmade cotton flannel coats sporting real goose-feather sprig trees. Antique Santa bells, dating back to the turn of the century are adorned with Dresden trims. A nine-inch wooden vintage "Skiing Santa" mechanical toy, created in late-1940s Germany, boasts arms that pump in unison with its skis. And blown-glass Santa ornaments, painted in frosty pastels, hail directly from the studios of contemporary German artists.

Blümchen collectibles are known for their details— so much so that an entire section of their catalog (dubbed "The Blümchen Gazette") is devoted to these finishing touches. Shoppers can purchase old-fashioned German Lametta tinsel roping, lacquered ornament caps from Poland, "old-time sparkles" (ground mica or diamond dust) from Germany, and Swedish tree candles. In addition, the company's warehouse is bursting with authentic crafting supplies the Boyces discovered throughout Europe.

"We feel like we're in a rabbit warren here," Diane says. "Fortunately, everyone has a good memory. We have forty two-gallon storage containers just filled with Dresdens," she continues. "We buy from companies going out of business and from lots of old German stores—that's where we can find cotton pipe cleaners, for example. I may have supplies or trims sitting around here for two or three years before I'm ready

Blümchen ornaments are known for their elaborate gold and silver glass trims.

to design the right ornament to use them. I have boxes of scrap paper with sketches on them."

Santa collectors also follow Blümchen's inventory of scrap-relief pictures, the forerunner of today's stickers. These vintage die cuts were especially popular in Victorian times as decorative elements and still are used today for decoupage projects, ornaments, and scrapbook pages. Although many of these Blümchen "scraps" originated in Germany in the 1800s, the company also sells reproductions.

IT'S ALL ABOUT THE HUNT

The Boyces replenish both their inventories and their creative juices with yearly treks to Germany. Typically, they spend most of each February traveling in both cities and countrysides in pursuit of the next perfect vintage mold, woolen felt, or classic crepe paper. They've become expert at the "cold call," paying countless visits to glassblowers, toy makers, and fabric shops. Armed with research, pictures, and Diane's "very bad German," the women succeed in securing spectacular new collectibles.

Always in pursuit of more off-beat items, Diane says the company's direction remains clear. "Everything we offer is something we'd love to have in our own homes," she explains. "If I wouldn't want to buy it myself, we don't offer it."✦

If you ask Bob Merck how this eclectic collection came to be, his answer is simple: "What I like to do is choose what appeals to me and things that I find interesting or rare." (From the collection of Bob Merck)

What exactly is it that inspires a Santa collection numbering hundreds of pieces? There are as many different answers as there are collectors, as you're about to discover.

DEVOTED COLLECTORS

Photograph by Perry Struse

A Kris Kringle Colony

SEATTLE-AREA SANTA HOBBYISTS HAVE LONG KNOWN THAT
THE QUAINT SHOP IN KIRKLAND OFFERS EXQUISITE CHRISTMAS
TREASURES. NOW IT'S FULL OF EVEN MORE REASONS TO BELIEVE.

Opposite: *The shop remains unique, thanks to its year-round commitment to producing and selling high-quality, one-of-a-kind Santas.*

Above: *"Black Peter," this signature piece, from carver Les Ramsey, was created from solid walnut. According to Scott Schultz, "Pieces like this come along only once in a great while."*

Tucked away on a quiet suburban street in Seattle sits a real-life Santa's workshop. Founded mostly on a dream six years ago by artist Dennis Brown and entrepreneur Scott Schultz, Reasons to Believe has grown from an exclusive gallery for their men's handcrafted Santas to one of the foremost associations of Santa artists. Selected craftspeople display and sell their work both on-line via the company's Web site (www.reasonstobelieve.com) and in the shop, offering a magnificent selection of one-of-a-kind Santas that numbers in the hundreds.

The tale of how the gallery began is almost as magical as the Santas it puts on display. Dennis had just moved to Seattle and was perched in a rented storefront window carving his winsome Santas from polymer clay. The president of Enesco Corporation happened to stroll by and liked what he saw.

Written by Debra Gibson ✦ *Photographs by Perry Struse*

Soon the company was reproducing Dennis's creations. Shortly after, Dennis and Scott were introduced at a mutual friend's Thanksgiving gathering. Before long, they knew they had what it would take to build their own Santa gallery, and the rest, as they say, is history.

As it's been from the beginning, the shop's specialty is the exquisitely detailed Santa figurines designed and crafted primarily by Dennis, often based on original ideas from Scott. Reasons to Believe holds fast to its original charge of creating and selling Santa items exclusively, and it can take from one week to several months to complete a piece to the men's satisfaction. Over the years, they've created more than seven hundred sculptures—so many that they've had to hire a full-time painter, Maurine Oates, to add much of the detailing.

About half of the shop's business comes from specially ordered pieces. A patriotic Santa was created for Vice President Dick Cheney's residence along with a Santa for the White House. The clay Santas range in style from traditional to folksy and may be as simple as a singular Old St. Nick or as elaborate as entire Yuletide scenes depicting "The Nutcracker" or "The Twelve Days of Christmas." The price tags run from about $500 for the former to $7,000 for the intricate signature pieces.

HANDS FOR THE HOLIDAYS

As the shop expands its inventory, more wood-carved Santas are joining the clay collections. About ten artists have affiliated with Reasons to Believe to market their wares. Those partnerships are established only after Dennis and Scott painstakingly review the artists' pieces and determine their compatibility with the gallery's existing inventory.

"All of the people we represent are committed not only to being Santa artists but also to making quality pieces," Scott explains. "Some of these artists may already have established outlets for their work, but I've yet to meet one who's so busy that he or she flat-out can't keep up. Any artist is always looking for a way to get in front of new people. You can live in a city of a half million people, and yet maybe only ten of them may collect what you make."

Wood carver Les Ramsey was the first new artist to join the Reasons to Believe fold. The Pennsylvania artist has long been revered as one of his craft's best exponents, and he has received numerous international carving awards. His walnut Santa faces, ranging in price from $350 to $750, are perennial favorites with collectors. But it is perhaps his towering "Black Peter" sculpture that has earned him the most fame. The twenty-two-inch statue, hand-carved from solid walnut, sells for $12,000.

Other carvers are leaving their mark on the gallery as well. Bob Dolata is an Iowa artisan whose Santas have a more rustic look, thanks to his signature use of cottonwood bark. Richard Nosiglia is an Oregon craftsman whose large carvings are initially sculpted

Above: *Scott Schultz and Dennis Brown, co-owners of Reasons to Believe, have cultivated a collector base that continues to double each year.*

Opposite: *With the inclusion of its new wood-carved works, Reasons to Believe boasts a gallery inventory of more than five hundred Santas.*

Reason
to Believ

Private Santa Colle
Sorry,
Not For Sale

For Sparklin

with a chain saw and then fine-tuned with smaller, more traditional hand tools. Mark Klein, an up-and-coming Midwestern artist, is creating a strong following with his elaborately detailed and diminutive (2–3-inch) carved wooden Santa faces. And Dave Francis, a Canadian carver who has garnered a strong world-wide following for his whimsical Santa characters, presents occasional carving shows and weekend exhibits at the gallery.

FROM RUSSIA WITH LOVE

To further establish itself as the home of "The World's Most Exclusive Santas," Reasons to Believe now sells figurines handcrafted by Russian and Ukrainian artists. Currently, five Russian artists produce high-quality painted signature pieces exclusively for the gallery. The handmade Santas from Ukraine, unique in style, are more reminiscent of folk-art chalkware.

To secure the pieces, Scott works through an intermediary. And in the true spirit of Christmas, he's nearly always surprised at what he receives. "What we get from these artists is never exactly what we might be expecting," Scott says. "There's always only one of each piece, and the carving and the painting often are totally different from what we asked for. But that's very exciting for our collectors, because these pieces are originals. They're very hard to find, and collectors typically leave our store with several of them."

Opposite and Lower Right: *Even though Reasons to Believe represents a range of artists, the shop's specialty is still the exquisitely detailed Santa figurines designed and crafted by Dennis. The Polar Express sculpture* opposite *spawned a limited-edition series. And the "signature" Santa at lower right is but one of nearly seven hundred that Dennis has created over the years.*

COLLECTORS KEEP COMING

It's that uniqueness that continues to lure collectors to the cozy gallery on Kirkland Avenue. "What separates us from the other shops in the country is that we do this year-round," Scott explains. "Our artists are actively working, and we continually promote and market their work every day of the year. To find a place where so many good artists are selling, under one roof, some of the most unique pieces anywhere in the world—I don't know that there *is* another like us.

"If there's a good Santa artist out there whom we don't know about, I'd be very surprised."✦

Stylish Santas

EACH CHRISTMAS, SANTA COLLECTOR GAIL FRASER OF SPARTA, NEW JERSEY, DECORATES HER TRADITIONAL HOME FROM FLOOR TO CEILING WITH COLORFUL, STYLISH SANTAS.

Opposite: Gail displays several beautiful ornament-laden trees throughout her home. Many of the trims are family heirlooms, but several Santa ornaments were gifts from guests.

Gail Fraser is adamant: "I begin decorating my house with Santas in early November," she says. "Of course, some of my largest Santas remain on display all year, but I pull most of the other pieces from boxes in the attic and place them around the house well before Thanksgiving."

A DECORATING TRADITION

When Gail first began collecting Santas, she always displayed a few of her favorite pieces during the holidays. But it wasn't until recently that she began to show them more formally in an annual holiday open house. "My Santa decorating grew dramatically one year when my church held a Christmas cookie-swap party," she says. "I volunteered to host the festivity and loaded my kitchen hearth with lots of my best Santas."

Many of her guests were fascinated by the stories Gail shared about the origins of the pieces. The following Christmas, the kitchen display spilled into every room of the house. "Now guests even bring Santa-ornament gifts to decorate the tree in my living room," she says.

Photographs by Tom McWilliam

But Gail's most prized Santas are the beautiful hand-made dolls she has received as gifts from her talented crafting friends. "Part of the joy of collecting Santas is knowing how each piece was made and who made it," she explains. "Every Santa you collect can have a unique story to go with it."

Her interpretive Santa dolls include a North woods trapper sporting a coonskin cap and a birch-bark canoe, an Old World gent wearing a crown of ever-greens and toting a Tannenbaum, and a fatherly figure ringing in the new year with a bell and cradling a baby angel asleep in his arms. A crafting friend named Faith often makes her own custom dolls. "If I can't find the special Santa I want," Gail says, "I can always count on Faith to make just what I'm looking for."

BALANCING THE DISPLAYS

In a house filled with so many Santas, is there any room left for other holiday decorations? You bet! "I move some furniture around to free a corner space just for snowmen," Gail says. Her special displays also include gingerbread man cookies on kitchen counters, red-and-green quilts draped on trunks or coffee tables, and buckets of ivory candles placed on hearths and windowsills. "I always replace my summer-white curtains and valances with holiday-theme burgundy window treatments."

Gail also treasures her collection of ceramic village pieces that decorates a table in her living room. Her husband, Alan, contributes his working antique American Flyer train set to the display, lending even more holiday charm.

SANTAS FOR EVERYONE

Gail loves to display Santas she has collected over a lifetime. There are examples that range from clothes-pin-size to six feet tall. Some are painted on wood, and others are fashioned from felt, cookie dough, clay, gourds, shells, and canvas. Some are egg-shaped; others are shaped like a crescent moon. Some wear coats of red, white, green, blue, or plaid. Still others are rendered in stained glass, crochet, and cross-stitch to hang on trees and garlands or serve as gift tags. There are Old World Santas and American folk-art versions. They appear in various guises, as bakers, golfers, and skiers.

Above: *Santa collector Gail Fraser fills her home with her latest discoveries as well as pieces she's gathered over a lifetime.*

Opposite: *A stair landing showcases a three-foot-tall Santa surrounded by other small Santa dolls and a generous display of greenery.*

Each Christmas, Gail's decorations take on fresh looks, as evidenced by these painted Santas in a variety of shapes and styles.

Opposite: Gail decorates her holiday table with ceramic Santa centerpieces and needlepoint Santa mini-stockings.

WELCOME HOME

"I collect Santas to decorate my home for myself and my family," Gail says, "but I also choose pieces that will make guests feel welcome in my home." Table settings at her holiday dinner parties include stenciled Santa place cards and mini-needlepoint Santa stockings as favors for guests. "It's all part of spreading more cheer," she says, "and that's what Santas do best!"✦

A Collectible
Christmas

FOR RITA AND STEVE CARNINE, OF ANKENY, IOWA, IT ALL STARTED
NEARLY FIFTEEN YEARS AGO, WHEN THE COUPLE FIRST BECAME
FASCINATED WITH AMERICAN COUNTRY ANTIQUES

Above: *A Santa steering his
sleigh is one of Rita and Steve's
most prized Christmas antiques.*

Opposite: *Decorated entirely with
antique ornaments—some from
Rita's childhood—the living room
tree is enclosed by a picturesque
doll-size picket fence that contains a
crowd of collectible toys and dolls.*

Rita especially became such a devoted fan that
in no time she had not only caught up with
but overtaken many veteran collectors, in
both the quantity and quality of her treasure trove.
Her Christmas collectibles alone are proof: more than
150 antique Santas; old dolls and toys by the hundreds,
numerous nineteenth-century German feather trees,
sleds—both adult-size and the quite rare doll-size—all
with their original paint, vintage lights and ornaments
and beads…you get the picture.

It's no coincidence that among the couple's huge
collection of country antiques Christmas pieces figure
so prominently. "Christmas is the big holiday for us,"
Rita says. "Winter is also my favorite time of year, so it
all comes together at the holidays."

Written by Candace Ord Manroe ✦ *Photographs by Perry Struse*

Rita and Steve are joined on their many collecting sojourns by their constant companion Alfie, a Maltese.

Opposite: An arrangement of dolls assumes Christmas significance when juxtaposed with a small tree. The two dolls in front are papier-mâché, the ones behind them rare oil-painted cloth dolls; and those on the tree are wooden peg dolls.

Below: Santas can be found all year long at the Carnines' house, including this candy container fellow who was once part of a department store display.

GETTING IN THE SPIRIT

Because she's a winter soul, Rita gravitates to cold-weather sports collectibles like antique sleds. With no specific Christmas connotation attached to them, the sleds work just fine displayed on her walls year-round. Then at Christmas, they become integrated into larger holiday-themed vignettes that include a sprinkling of Santas and freshly cut evergreen boughs. Rita's advice: Work with what you have, and try to see the holiday-decorating potential in even non-Christmas collectibles. Adding just a sprig or two of greenery can make any display of collectibles suddenly jolly with holiday cheer.

Old toys and dolls are some of Rita's other favorite collectibles that are richly vested with holiday-decorating possibilities. Christmas simply gives her an excuse to bring them out of the bedrooms for display, en masse, in the main rooms of her home. Certainly the family's old-fashioned Christmas tree wouldn't be the same without them, its base fringed with the friendly faces of beloved bunnies, timeworn teddy bears, and quaintly clothed dolls. "I love collecting toys and dolls. I guess I never grew up," says Rita, who's grateful for the opportunity to indulge her passion at Christmas.

Rita's most interesting seasonal displays often are a combination of year-round and Christmas collectibles. For example, at Christmas, rows of dolls that stand on

At the turn of a key, this late-1800s German feather tree revolves and plays a medley of Christmas carols—features that make it an especially prized collectible.

display all year beneath an architectural shelf are joined by a small tree ornamented with still more dolls—this time, the wooden peg variety. Even the shelf above the dolls takes on the holiday spirit with a garland of greenery and two small wreaths.

In the past, Rita proudly displayed a few of her special Santas year-round. But these days, with their numbers ever growing, there are just too many to showcase. Storing them in closets and on shelves until mid-November is her strategy for sanity. Then, for the holidays, they switch places with her other collectibles, and the house once again brims with Santas, reindeer, and other yuletide treasures.

"How much decorating we do really depends on how much entertaining we plan that year," Rita says. During one recent Christmas, in addition to celebrating with their four grown sons and their families, the Carnines hosted a Christmas party for their local Quester chapter, a historical group that researches a local area's history. With Rita and Steve's Christmas collectibles decorating every nook and cranny, the Questers found plenty to appreciate.✦

One corner of the living room is decorated with late-1800s sleds still sporting their original paint. For Christmas, Rita has favorite miniature Santas posing sled-side. To the right of the full-size sleds, she displays some very rare doll sleds, which manufacturers gave to lucky children to match their own newly purchased sleds.

Opposite: *Two new Iowa-crafted Santas make a riveting focal point, the larger one standing nearly six feet tall. Rita specially commissioned it, incorporating her own 1906 vintage quilt as clothing and tiny antique toys as trims. The smaller Santa also carries antique toys.*

X'mas comes but once a year

MERRY CHRISTMAS

Merry Christmas,
dearest friend,
As Santa Claus
can make it!
And every chance,
Mirth and Fun,
Be wise,
in time,
and
take it

An Antique Christmas

DECORATIONS FROM THE TURN OF THE TWENTIETH CENTURY—
THE MORE UNUSUAL, THE BETTER—CHARM THIS CHRISTMAS
COLLECTOR. SANTA CLAUS STARS IN YEAR-ROUND DISPLAYS
THROUGHOUT BOB MERCK'S HOME.

*Opposite: Groupings of favorite
antique Santa collectibles add
interest throughout Bob's home.*

B ob Merck's obsession started innocently enough.
While scouting for antique clocks and furniture, the
Connecticut attorney spied a pair of Christmas
lightbulbs—the old-fashioned kind that screw into a
string of lights. Made of painted milk glass and shaped
like a parrot and a Santa Claus, the 1930s Japanese lights
cost just five dollars for the two of them.

"I remember my grandparents had a few of these on
their tree," Bob says. "It brought back a lot of memories
for me." Now, some twenty years later, Bob owns more
than one thousand figural Christmas lights. "That
five-dollar purchase proved to be quite expensive," he
concedes with a laugh.

Bob's Christmas cache soon grew to include antique
ornaments, toys, and Santa Clauses of every description.
He doesn't even know how many Christmas items he
has amassed. "My goal isn't to have one of everything
ever made," says Bob, who showcased his collection in
the 1992 book *Deck the Halls: Treasures of Christmas Past.*
"What I like to do is choose what appeals to me and
things that I find interesting or rare."

Written by Kellye Carter Crocker ✦ *Photographs by Perry Struse*

A CHRISTMAS FAMILY

Bob appreciates family Christmas traditions. His own 1950s childhood Christmases in Oregon were enchanting, and the holidays still star as his favorite time of year.

"When I was small, my parents put great effort into making Christmas a wonderful time for the family," he says. Most years, they allowed Bob and his younger brother, Tim, to decorate their own miniature Christmas tree in their bedroom. "We thought it was spectacular, although if we could go back and see it now, we'd probably laugh," says Bob, who was only four or five when the tradition began.

While Bob grew up to become a master Christmas collector, Tim, his only sibling, started Merck Family's Old World Christmas with his wife Beth. The Spokane, Washington, company makes and sells ornaments and collectibles in the old European style. "My brother and I are such Christmas enthusiasts, our parents have been accused of dropping us on our heads on Christmas Eve when we were small," Bob says with a chuckle.

THE "FIRST GOOD GERMAN SANTA"

Bob owns hundreds of Santas, most of them handcrafted in Germany from the 1860s through the 1920s. "When you think of Santa Claus, most people smile," he says. "He's really a mythic figure, and he's such an integral part of Christmas for most of us."

Bob's voice rings with excitement as he recalls buying his "first good German Santa" years ago. He willingly paid the fifteen-dollar asking price to an elderly woman who was selling some of her parents' holiday decorations. The stern Santa, circa 1900–1910 and in excellent condition, wears a red and green mohair coat that hides a cylinder for holding candy.

Two years later, the woman's brother called. He wanted to sell the rest of their parents' collection. "He was very happy," Bob says. "He knew their family decorations would be back together."

Above Left: *Bob Merck, a lawyer and author, re-creates the magic of his childhood Christmases with hundreds of antique Santa toys and collectibles throughout his Connecticut home.*

This is the papier-mâché German Santa from the early 1900s that led Bob to serious Santa collecting.

Opposite: *Bob displays portions of his collection throughout his home year-round, including these stern-faced German Belsnickle Santas. Bob, who has traveled to Germany several times, says it's easier to find antique German Santas in the United States.*

These Japanese milk-glass Christmas lights from the 1930s launched Bob's Christmas collection in 1980. Now he owns more than one thousand figural lights alone.

YEAR-ROUND DISPLAY

No matter what the season, Bob showcases Christmas collectibles throughout his home, a former mill built in 1734. In one room, custom-built floor-to-ceiling lighted cabinets shelter an array of holiday figures. Santas wear robes in every color imaginable, including purple, yellow, orange, and gray. Father Christmas can be seen riding a horse, a donkey, and even an elephant. Bob found the elephant rider at an antique show in New Jersey—still wrapped in newspaper from 1901.

Turn-of-the-twentieth-century Santa board games feature detailed lithography. In one of Bob's favorite games, players try to get Santa to bypass their neighbor's house so they can reap more presents themselves. "I think that's really a riot," he says.

Lighted shelves in the great room spotlight more of his collection, such as groupings of small bisque Santas from the early 1900s. Each little Santa is busy—stuffing a crying boy into a bag, climbing a fence, flying an open-air airplane, rowing a boat, driving a stagecoach, or talking on a hand-cranked telephone. Jigsaw puzzles, wooden blocks, and even a child's silver pocketknife carry St. Nick's image.

A Victorian bowl-and-pitcher set shows Santa loaded down with toys and prized oranges. "I'm very intrigued with what the original owners must have been like to have had something of this quality and size just for Christmas," Bob says. "Every piece has a story behind it."

Other favorites include a wooden ladder toy from the 1880s made by the Bliss Company in Connecticut; and a lithographed paper image of a hot-air balloon with reindeer peeking over the edge of the basket as Santa ratchets down the ladder, drops into a chimney, and pops out of the fireplace at the bottom. Then there's the stern Belsnickle, circa 1900, dressed in a white robe and holding a feather tree, that multitasks as a decorative

figure, a candy box, and a candleholder. And don't forget the wooden pull toy from the 1890s that features Santa sidesaddle on a sled driven by two reindeer. Bob marvels that the artist took the time to make the running reindeer different from each other. "They're very animated and very realistic," he says.

COLLECTING TODAY

When Bob began collecting, antique dealers typically kept their Christmas pieces boxed up until the holidays. Since Christmas collecting boomed in the last decade, dealers now peddle Santas and similar items year-round. Competition has stiffened, however. "You have to search far and wide to find things," Bob says, "but the chase is a lot of fun."

Bob understands why this type of collecting appeals to so many people. It's the same force that drew him to those two Christmas lightbulbs years ago. "I think Christmas collectors strive to re-create the Christmases they remember," Bob says simply. "We may act like adults, but inside we're all kids."✦

Opposite: *This moonfaced German squeak toy, from about 1890, is one of Bob's favorite old Christmas toys. The two-sided toy has a moon face on one side and the face of Little Red Riding Hood on the reverse. Between the two faces is patterned fabric that conceals a spring mechanism.*

In Victorian times, a wash set used only during the Christmas season would have seemed extravagant. Among the brown-robed Santa's treats are juicy, rare oranges. The standing Santa behind the wash set was originally a display piece in an old German bakery. He was placed in the window during the holidays to attract customers and held freshly baked treats in his basket.

MASTER CRAFTERS

Prepare to be amazed.
You're about to meet eight
talented artisans for whom
Santa Claus is a true inspiration.
Whether he's rendered in
wood, clay, fabric, or paint,
the results are magical.

*A hand gently sheltering a white dove—this detail
from Anne Chase Sanregret's "Santa of the Snows"
speaks volumes about its subject and its creator.*

Photograph by Perry Struse

Unveiling Beauty

FIRMLY ROOTED IN HIS FAMILY'S REVERENCE FOR HISTORIC HOMES, BRADLEY BRUINSMA HAS CREATED HIS OWN UNIQUE WAY OF RESTORING LIFE TO THE PAST.

Above: When he first began creating his Spindlenicks, Bradley Bruinsma started with antique bedposts and railings. He now carves many of his own spindles from scratch.

Unveiling hidden beauty from unlikely places has been a lifetime endeavor for Hoosier artist Bradley Bruinsma. When he's in his studio, he enjoys exploring art in a variety of media. But his sincerest passion is an art form that often goes unrecognized: the art of carving wooden spindles. What began as a pastime of transforming antique bedposts, staircase railings, and porch spindles into vintage Santas has transformed into Bradley's own unique business, Spindlenicks.

"It is all too easy to waste vast amounts of time coveting beautiful things that are out of reach," Bradley says. "A much greater joy comes from learning to tap into and appreciate the beauty that is already around you."

Written by Bradley O'Bryan Hawks ✦ *Photographs by Craig Anderson*

From old neglected wooden spindles, Bradley creates Spindlenicks that are full of fresh holiday spirit.

CARRYING ON A TRADITION

Born and raised in Lafayette, Indiana, Bradley grew up with a mother and father who enjoyed restoring century-old homes to their original beauty. Carrying on the family tradition and then living in a renovated home from the early 1800s, he soon discovered his own unique way to breathe new life into treasures from the past—his timeless wooden Santas.

"Ten winters ago, I was standing in an old home Mom and Dad were working on, just resting my arm on the staircase and reflecting on how Christmas has always been the most cherished time of year in our home," Bradley recalls. "I looked down at the staircase I was leaning on, silently admiring the dedication it took to handcraft the spindles in the railing, and an idea hit me."

I thought, "How tragic that such beauty has been taken for granted and left to deteriorate!" It seemed to Bradley that each of those spindles had its own personality and a two-hundred-year history to be discovered. Bradley took a spindle from the staircase and gave it a face in the likeness of Santa Claus—an endearing family symbol of tradition, benevolence, and fellowship.

Each Spindlenick is born from a spindle unique in
shape, height, and width.

Opposite: Bradley creates his Spindlenicks from every
imaginable type of spindle. Some are freestanding,
some are designed to hang as ornaments, and others
are crafted as table or floor lamps.

A PERSONAL RENAISSANCE

That staircase spindle was the beginning of a new art form for Bradley. Still in his possession, it has been the inspiration for more than a thousand Spindlenicks he has since created. The simple restoration of a neglected piece of architecture has bloomed into a year-round labor of love. To Bradley, it seemed only natural that he should share that love with those around him.

"I started taking some of my Spindlenicks to a local store in Lafayette, just to see if others would find in them the same joy I had." Almost immediately, he attracted an enthusiastic group of collectors who now request his Spindlenicks each Christmas.

Each Spindlenick starts out as some form of spindle. Sometimes the spindles are from old bedposts, staircases, chairs, tables, or even lamps. More recently, Bradley has taken his art one step further and begun to carve his own spindles. "It's my personal conviction to appreciate the art in all the spindles I find. So it seemed only natural that I should try to keep that art alive by creating spindles of my own."

A METICULOUS PROCESS

With his vintage spindles, Bradley starts by removing any paint, coatings, or buildup that may have accumulated over the years. Then he sands the base of the spindle so it can stand on its own. Next he applies several coats of paint—always in the richest colors he can develop and often with a marble, wash, or other classic finish. Then he paints a face on the spindles, each one unique in eye color, hair, beard, spectacles, and a myriad of other features. Finally he adds finishing touches of trim, holly leaves, elves, and other fanciful ornamentation. "I love finding a spindle with a knot out of it or a little imperfection. Imperfections give a spindle character," Bradley says. Sometimes, he paints angelic eyes peeking out from within a nick in the spindle.

The spindles Bradley carves himself have a beauty of their own; reminiscent of old spindles, they allow him the freedom to experiment with designs. Whether his spindles are old or new, he finishes off every unique Spindlenick in each edition by hand-signing, dating, and numbering it. Depending upon the degree of ornamentation and the intensity of the paint colors, a Spindlenick can take up to forty hours to complete.

Bradley loves sharing his gift. "I've been doing this for ten years, and I never dreamed I'd have collectors calling each year. It just thrills me that others find the joy of the season in my Spindlenicks," he declares. Bradley sells his Spindlenicks primarily through local stores and by mail. For the future, he plans to expand his market, staying in touch with his creativity and developing new editions to bring even more joy to his collectors. "I love looking at my Spindlenicks from the first few years and seeing creations that stemmed from antique beauty. Looking ahead to future editions, I'm eager to continue designing my own spindles, carrying on a rich tradition for those after me to enjoy."✦

Some Spindlenicks are designed to hang on a doorknob rather than stand on a mantel. But what they all have in common is a reflection of the past hidden in the unique history of each spindle.

Opposite: The first step in the meticulous process of creating new Spindlenicks involves stripping any paint or finish from the spindles.

Front Porch Santas

IN AN ALABAMA NEIGHBORHOOD KNOWN FOR ITS
GRACIOUS VICTORIAN HOMES, DISPLAY ARTIST JAN JONES TURNS
FRONT PORCHES INTO STORYBOOK SHOWCASES FOR SANTA.

*Above: Jan Jones with one of her best-known porch
Santas, a six-footer dressed in red water taffeta with
gold lamé trim. His distinctive face has appeared in
brochures about the front porch displays.*

Nine years ago, Jan Jones of Opelika, Alabama, had
an interesting problem: what to do with a surplus
of life-size Santa statues. She'd sculpted and
costumed half a dozen six-foot papier-mâché Santas for
a local mall, but they weren't needed immediately, and
the mall management asked her to store them for a year.
Jan, a floral designer and display artist, couldn't bear to
see her Santas gathering dust in her studio during the
holidays. So, gazing around the North Opelika Historic
Neighborhood that she calls home, she realized that
nearly every one of the stately houses had a substantial
front porch. In her mind's eye, she envisioned a holiday
tableau on each porch, complete with a Santa figure,
props, garlands, and twinkling lights.

Written by Allison Engel ✦ *Photographs by Craig Anderson*

...tags, boxes and match color. On this
seated Santa were chosen to complement the trim
on this vintage home on North Eighth Street.
Jan has the Santas stand or sit to fit the
proportions of each home and porch.

Merry
Christmas
Love
SANTA

"We have very pretty porches here," Jan says, and she should know. The self-taught artist and her husband Bill have lived in an 1896 Victorian beauty for nearly twelve years. "Our houses have kept a lot of their old heritage. We have the most intact Victorian neighborhood in Alabama."

Jan suggested the idea at a neighborhood meeting. With the assistance of her mother, Roberta Westmark (whom Jan describes as "a ninety-three-year-old wonder"), and helpful friends, the group created Victorian Christmas displays on six porches, using props and decorations Jan had on hand from her business. The tableaux were an immediate hit, and soon neighborhood residents were walking and driving from house to house to admire the decorations.

THE FRONT PORCH VOLUNTEERS

The next summer, a group of about a dozen women from the neighborhood came to Jan's studio to help make twelve Santas to replace the ones she finally delivered to the mall. Thus was born the Victorian Front Porch Christmas Tour. Nine years later, the tour has grown to include nearly fifty turn-of-the-century homes on two streets in the neighborhood, encompassing an area of ten blocks.

Every summer, the dedicated neighborhood volunteers help make more six-foot Santas, carousel horses, and elves to keep up with the demand from porch owners. The viewing takes place Wednesday through Sunday in early to mid-December. On Saturday night, the streets are closed to vehicles, and visitors walk from house to house, entertained by sixty or so volunteers dressed in Victorian costumes. Some costumes are rented; others are improvised after trips to flea markets and garage sales for old formals and wedding gowns. Anyone willing to dress up is welcome to join the fun. "We let anyone who wants to play with us come out and get a costume," Jan says. The ladies in lace and bustles and the men in top hats and velvet are joined by school choirs singing

This bust of a Santa, with a red brocade robe and a face hand-sculpted by Jan, is part of a mantel display in her showroom.

Opposite: *A three-foot Santa holding a tree wired with tiny lights beckons visitors into the showroom area of Jan's studio, where other handcrafted Santas are displayed.*

A papier-mâché tree stump topped with a lantern lights the way for this Santa, robed in a rich tapestry fabric. He stands twenty-eight inches tall.

Opposite: *This four-and-half-foot Santa, dressed in a red water taffeta and gold lamé robe, stands ready to greet visitors. Everything from the robe to the carousel horse, which is made from plaster and papier-mâché and then painted gold, is hand-formed by Jan and her small army of volunteers.*

carols, a theatre troupe presenting excerpts from holiday plays, and a bell choir playing seasonal melodies. Hot wassail is served in a historic neighborhood home, where a storyteller holds forth to the delight of all.

At some homes the decorations spill out onto the front lawn. The Christmas displays might include a vintage sleigh or even a reindeer pulling a buggy made from bicycle wheels and refrigerator parts. Homeowners add to the ambience by lighting candles in their windows, hanging wreaths on their doors, and twining red ribbons and garlands through their porch railings. Figures of carolers are posed with gingerbread houses and gingerbread men. Old-fashioned toys surround elves, and Santas hold lanterns and decorative walking sticks.

Opelika, only five miles from Auburn and Auburn University, has embraced the porch tour as a way to capitalize on preservation efforts in the historic town. Twice the tour has been recognized as one of the "Top 20 Events in the Southeast" by the Southeast Tourism Society. Another plus is that the hardworking neighbors have become fast friends while staging the event. "When it's not raining, it's magical," Jan says. "It rained three years in a row, and that was tough."

JAN'S CREATIONS EXPAND

For a quarter of a century, Jan has been in the Santa business, creating and selling small papier-mâché Santas with hand-sculpted and hand-painted clay faces. Her sixteen-inch Old World Santas, which retail for about one hundred dollars, are her most popular items and sell out every year. Her expanded repertoire now includes snowmen, Nativity figures, and angels for Christmas as well as chicks, ducks, and rabbits for Easter. From the small retail shop in the front of her studio in downtown Opelika, fans of Creations by Jan—located in a mid-1800s building that formerly housed a hardware store, bakery, and pool hall—seek out her Jan Jones originals to add to their collections.

Jan also sells larger figures, charging about one hundred dollars per foot. The life-size figures have a chicken-wire base and are covered with fabric dipped in plaster. Working like a stage-set designer, she says, "Anything underneath is fair game. Everything is hot-glued down, and all that matters is what you see on the outside."

The exterior fabrics are rich taffetas, brocades, and metallics, all dipped in wallpaper paste for stiffness. "I like long, 'drapey' fabrics, and faces with a pensive look," Jan says. She uses a lot of greenery, grapevines, and silk flowers on her creations and often electrifies her figures by weaving tiny white lights among the flora and fauna.

All the porches are returned to normal the Monday morning following the tour period. A local construction company volunteers its staff to help dismantle the scenes and transport the figures. Another local company donates warehouse space to store the decorations from year to year.

Each summer, there always seems to be more work to do—embellishing, repairing, and fine-tuning the displays. "When I'm surrounded by everything half-finished in the fall, I never think we'll make it," Jan says. "But I just take my vitamins and keep on trucking."✦

Above: *As befits her background in floral design, Jan often mixes wreaths and Santa faces. These Santa head wreaths were designed for doors, walls, or mantels. Each Santa wears a red taffeta headpiece with ribbon trim and bells.*

Opposite: *A whimsical Santa holds a hot-air balloon on this grand front porch as three tiny elves, also made by Jan, scamper about.*

In the Nick of Time

NICHOLAS BOLLENBACH ISN'T YOUR TYPICAL TEENAGER.
STAYING UP LATE AT NIGHT TO PAINT HIS VISIONS OF SANTA, THIS
EAGER YOUNG ARTIST CREATES IMAGES OF HOPE AND INSPIRATION.

*Above: At just eighteen years old,
Nicholas Bollenbach can look forward
to years of painting Santas. "I'm taking
orders one day at a time," he says about
his business, Prairie Art Originals.*

*Opposite: This Jolly Old St. Nick,
the first in a series of one hundred
limited-edition originals, was featured in
Country Home magazine. The smaller
Santa paintings and dolls are one-of-a-kind
products of Nick's imagination.*

Eighteen-year-old Nicholas Bollenbach sits hunched over a canvas at the kitchen table in his suburban Minneapolis, Minnesota, home. Surrounded by hundreds of crimped acrylic paint tubes, he searches for the perfect shades of gray and blue to highlight Santa's beard. Forget about girls, cars, and books—this is Nick's time to dream and paint.

With their simple lines and familiar themes, Nick's primitive paintings express a certain innocence. One proud St. Nick waves the Stars and Stripes; another serves as a perch for a folk-art bird. Nick paints whatever comes to mind, rarely planning his colorful scenes but still knowing exactly what he wants to achieve. "I'm involved in art because it's my passion," he says simply.

Written by Judith Stern Friedman ✦ Photographs by Craig Anderson

Painting this famous couple came naturally—Nick had created similar pairs of Santa rag dolls and samplers. He referred to a magazine clipping of an old woman to shape his vision of Mrs. Claus.

Opposite: *Nick often uses folk-art figures to embellish his paintings, such as the bird shown with this Father Christmas. The fabric Santa doll also is one of Nick's creations, which he stitched completely by hand at age fourteen.*

Already this young man is crafting his future, building a business one painting at a time. Nick is the only member of the family who paints. His dad is a security officer, his mom an interior designer, and his married older brother, Chris, a songwriter. In four years, Nick has established Prairie Art Originals, named after the family's previous street address. Despite school, home, and social demands, he always finds time to render his visions of Santa and express the warmth and wonder of the season.

"Christmas is my favorite time of year," Nick explains. "Our family is so busy, but at Christmas we can come together for a while."

WORKING FROM HEAD AND HEART

Recently moving from Faribault, Minnesota, to the family's Apple Valley townhome and leaving many of his friends behind, Nick appreciates his family ties more now than ever. But he still looks forward to his time alone. "My art lets me do something by myself," he says. "Sometimes I'll be up late at night and pick up the brush and paint for two or three hours." When he has an idea, Nick works from his head: "I just get a feeling for it."

Nick also relies on an album he has compiled full of images from postcards, magazines, holiday cards, fabrics, and anything else that inspires him. "I'm not tied to any particular style," he says. "If I see one idea, I can think of a whole bunch of different ways to paint it."

Describing his work as whimsical and folklike, Nick has painted almost every kind of Santa there is, from the modern-day jolly old man to the stern-looking Father Christmas of old.

Working on wood or canvas, Nick paints one-of-a-kind originals as small as 5×7 inches and as large as 2×4 feet. "I usually start by doing a face," he says. "Instead of painting the beard white, I mix in a lot of different colors to make it more textured." He finishes his wood paintings with an antique frame and leaves his canvases with painted edges. On both, he applies an antique glaze to give his work an aged appearance.

MAGIC IN THE MAKING

Nick's mother, Bobbie, is perhaps his biggest fan. When Nick was five years old, he was Bobbie's "little shadow," doodling superheroes while Bobbie did needlework for her business, the Prairie Sampler. By age eight, Nick was sewing his own samplers and rag dolls. He even whip-stitched a Santa Claus onto a scrap of linen. "I became such a perfectionist," Nick laughingly recalls, "the whole picture had to be covered."

By nine years old, he was selling samplers at Country Porch Antiques in Burnsville, Minnesota, where his mother also had a business. Then he sent needlework samples to a family friend, Mary Turek. "Mary bought everything I made," Nick says. Although his stitching was beautiful, it was also time-consuming, and Nick quickly burned out from all the repetition. "Painting opened up a whole new way to use my creativity," he explains.

When Nick was thirteen years old, Mary Turek bought his first horse painting, as well as subsequent renditions of dogs, farm animals, and garden scenes. Then she suggested that Nick try holiday themes, which he also offered to Country Porch Antiques. At the shop's Christmas Open House, all twenty of his paintings sold out. A mention that same year in the holiday issue of *Country Home* magazine (November/December) only added to his growing fame.

Nick officially started his business at age fifteen, but was too young to retain legal control, so his mother helped him manage the finances. "I like the fact that Nick's an entrepreneur," Bobbie says. "He goes out, finds something he needs to do, and he does it."

RISING STAR

Today, Nick paints on demand and promotes his work through direct mail. And, to make more efficient use of his time, he's considering selling limited-edition prints. Surprisingly, Nick has no formal art training—only the artistic influence of his mother and occasional coaching from his grandfather, William Olson. "Grandpa used to sketch photos of our toys," he remembers. "If I was

drawing something, he would explain where to put the shadows." Nick admits that his interest is inborn. Even at his part-time job at a movie theater, he finds himself doodling on the backs of the ticket stubs.

When he's not painting, Nick is a typical teenager who enjoys cars, his friends, and acting—but everyone who knows him agrees that he's extraordinary. He volunteers at an area humane society, has won awards for his outstanding writing, and has stolen the show in school plays. He hopes to pursue the arts in college. "It's a bit ironic that his name is Nicholas," his mother says. She's convinced that in the spirit of his namesake, there's a touch of magic in him.✦

Nick's patriotic Santas appeal to folks who want to display them year-round. The traditional American Santa shown here proudly waves the flag.

Opposite: *On this scenic sampler, Nick experimented by adding an alphabet and borders to the Santa in the snow. Above it, whimsical, gnomelike Santas are reminiscent of early folk art.*

Woolly Wonders

DONNA LOVELADY IS HOOKED ON SANTA.
HER WARMING DOLLS MAKE A SPIRITED STAND IN WOOL.

Above: At age fifty-nine, Donna is always working on new hooked projects and patterns. "I devour everything I can find on crafts and interior design," she says.

Opposite: Rosy cheeks, deep dark eyes, and faces full of wholesome, curly wool make Donna's Santas particularly expressive.

Donna Lovelady insists that her Santas make themselves. "I'm just the person who hooks them," she says. With their innocent eyes, simple dress, and billowy beards, each rousing Santa has a life of its own. Beards of natural uncarded sheep's wool hint at the warmth that lies beneath. Coats are lovingly hooked, not stitched, a technique that differentiates Donna's Santas from many similar dolls. She considers her characters primitive in style, though their realistic eyes always convey a hopeful, warm human expression.

"I've always loved Christmas," Donna says. "It brings back happy memories of my childhood." She fondly recalls spending early Christmas Eves at the neighbors', then returning home to discover that Santa had visited.

Written by Judith Stern Friedman ✦ *Photographs by Perry Struse*

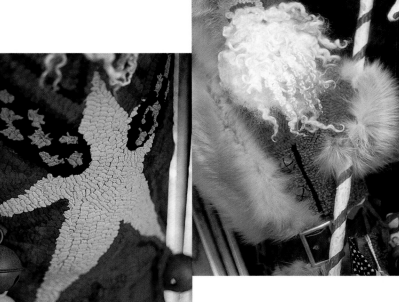

EVOLVING VISIONS

Today, Santa continues to visit Donna at her Napa, California, home; only now he comes by way of her imagination. "I wake up in the middle of the night with these ideas," she explains. "Everything I see triggers an idea for something." Her garage is a physical extension of her mind, crowded with countless hunted treasures such as old wool scraps, twigs, bells, and fur that someday will become another notion for St. Nick. "I've taken over the garage with all my stuff," Donna says. She also keeps a scrapbook for cataloging her ideas, which she claims already are plentiful enough to last for the rest of her life.

To create her dolls, Donna starts with recycled Salvation Army wool coats, which she cleans, dyes, and then cuts into quarter-inch strips. Starting with a burlap-type backing called monk's cloth, she draws a pattern to be hooked, then loops in the wool strips accordingly. After sewing up the back, she fills the form with cat litter and stuffing, adding more weight at the bottom to stabilize it.

Bells, old belts, fur, and other accessories transform the hooked shapes into particular personalities. When all the little details are completed, Donna glues the beard on last. Some may say that the authentic curly sheep's wool makes her Santas look a bit disheveled, but Donna thinks it just makes them all the more endearing.

When Donna's not crafting, she shops crafts fairs, flea markets, and estate sales seeking inspiration from old-fashioned things. Her most recent finds are antique war medals she says will be perfect for her men of honor.

Above: *"I try to give the eyes a realistic look," Donna explains, "like human eyes, with irises and highlights." Donna hooks the entire body and face, then adds uncarded sheep's wool for the beard.*

Opposite: *Tall, skinny Santas are weighted with cat litter to keep them from toppling. The 4-foot-tall Santa in the foreground dons a fox fur cape and carries a papier-mâché candy cane. Behind him, the fifty-seven-inch stovepipe Santa is warmed by a sixteen-inch-long lamb's-wool beard.*

Donna's whimsical papier-mâché creations are wool-hooked Santa predecessors. This patriotic spirit bears a sack full of toys from crafts shows, thrift shops, and flea markets.

FEEDING THE PASSION

"I love hooking more than anything I've ever done in crafts," Donna says. Because her Santas take from two weeks to a month to create, "It wouldn't be feasible to sell them," she explains. Rather, Donna and her friend Robin Kingsley started Woolsworth in the fall of 2001 to sell their wool-hooked Santa patterns, penny rugs, and wool appliqué designs, which they hope someday to distribute internationally.

Donna is always busy doing something. "I never seem to stop and just sit," she says. Besides rug hooking, which is her first love, she coordinates an annual holiday crafts show called Just Be Claus. As an organizer and participant in the show for the past ten years, she's sold everything from custom wreaths and floral arrangements to painted accents and papier-mâché Santas. Only in the last few years has she added her hooked Santas, rugs, and pillows, and at every show, they've sold out.

"Hooking is becoming a very popular craft now," Donna explains. She hooks at night while her husband watches television and is glad to be doing something with her hands while keeping him company. Donna also teaches rug-hooking classes at Three Sisters, a crafts and home-decor shop in Sonoma, California, and is currently writing a book on first-time rug hooking.

LONG-TERM TALENT

Donna says her work is always evolving. "If I don't like something, I adjust it." That flexibility comes from years of crafting as a child. Growing up, Donna made fabric clothes for her paper dolls. Her mother and grandmother also sewed the family's clothes, and Donna naturally followed their lead, learning to sew on a treadle machine and honing her skills in home economics classes.

School led to marriage and then a sales manager job in northern California for a Dallas-based home accessories company, where Donna worked for twenty-five years. When she retired in 1990, she filled her time with tole-painting classes and the crafts she made to sell at Just Be Claus. She first latched onto rug hooking when she saw a picture of a hooked stool seat cover in a magazine. With no accessible classes in Napa, Donna organized a group of women and enlisted rug hooker Nancy Miller to teach them the technique. Since then, Donna has hooked at every opportunity, although she still enjoys a variety of other crafts, designing new projects and sharing them with the people she loves.

With her husband John (who works at the Oakland, California, district attorney's office), seven grown sons, and ten grandchildren—all within a 50-mile radius—Donna enjoys a large support group and lives up to her Lovelady name. Just as Santa does when he visits, Donna leaves a memorable impression.✦

Donna hooked this "Just Be Claus"
pillow for the annual crafts show she coordinates.
There she and four other crafts enthusiasts feature the
work of about thirty-five different artists.

Honest Pots

RON GARFINKEL IS A MAN OF THE EARTH. HIS UNPRETENTIOUS SALT-GLAZED POTTERY SPEAKS NOT ONLY OF HIS TALENT BUT ALSO OF HIS HUMANITY.

Above: *"I take a lot of my inspiration from the wildlife around me," says Monroe Salt Works owner and founder Ron Garfinkel.*

Opposite: *Some people describe Ron's style as Victorian because of his pieces' rustic finishes and delicate transfers. These stern-faced Santas in fur-trimmed robes stand poised upon earth-tone clay, reminiscent of their rural European origins.*

In an old chicken barn in Monroe, Maine (about 15 miles north of Belfast), residents use their hands to turn out more than twelve hundred pieces of pottery a week. Employing the same salt-glazing techniques as their colonial American ancestors, these craftspeople celebrate a return to simplicity, which shows through in every splendid piece they make.

HANDSOME HANDWORK

Welcome to the world of Monroe Salt Works, whose mastermind, founder, and designer, Ron Garfinkel, invests his life and livelihood in his pottery. "Our pieces are straightforward and utilitarian," he explains. Their generous lips, functional handles, and bold designs reflect a practical yet artistic sensibility. His traditional Santa images are the perfect embodiment of rustic Victoriana, and the shapely holly branches, pine trees, crows, and other decorative elements reflect Ron's appreciation of the natural world.

Written by Judith Stern Friedman ✦ *Photographs by Perry Struse*

Most of Ron's pieces are hand-painted and stenciled; others boast beautiful ceramic transfers (similar to decals but using glaze instead of ink). These last often are applied to utilitarian dishes such as mugs, plates, chowder bowls—everything that would be considered part of a place setting," Ron says.

Remarkably, each piece is handled up to eighteen times by twelve different people who perform different operations. They mix the clay, run it through a pug mill (to remove the air), bat it out to make it flat, and then mold it, trim it, decorate it, clean it, glaze it, wax it (to resist the glaze), and load and unload the kiln. Then the bottoms are ground and sanded, and the finished pieces are packaged for shipping. Depending on the weather, the entire process may take anywhere from one to two weeks, and no two pieces ever look the same.

POTS WITH PERSONALITY

"People are attracted to our pottery because some pieces are light and some pieces are dark," Ron explains. "By nature, salt-glazed pieces don't match." The gray-colored clay is Ron's own recipe, made from seven different

ingredients and refined over the years for its color, heat resistance, and workability. Most pieces are shaped using plaster molds based on pieces he first throws by hand.

The banded pottery is painted before firing by turning it on a potter's wheel; for other pieces, like the Santa collection, German-made lithographic transfers are applied after one firing and then fired again to fuse the image onto the base glaze.

In either case, the salt-glazing process takes place during firing. Physically throwing handfuls of rock salt into the white-hot kiln at the peak of firing creates a chemical reaction with the silica in the clay to produce a wide range of colors and textures, depending on where the piece sits in the kiln. "The variation is what makes the whole body of work so rich," Ron says. Although he finds

Above: Each Monroe Salt Works piece is handled up to eighteen times by as many as twelve different people. No two pots are ever the same.

Opposite: A multitude of tools are used to mold, trim, decorate, clean, glaze, and wax the pottery before the pieces are loaded into the kiln.

Opposite: *Up to five hundred pieces of pottery can be fired at a time. Each one is carefully and methodically placed in the kiln, according to the desired finish.*

Below: *A base-coat glaze on Santa mugs establishes a surface to which the transfers can adhere.*

it difficult to compete with mass-marketed pottery, he's happy that his work is distinguished by its one-of-a-kind craftsmanship and design.

Today, Monroe Salt Works encompasses not only a twelve-person studio and wholesale business but also administrative and retail operations in five locations: Arlington, Massachusetts; Lahaska, Pennsylvania; Belfast, Ellsworth, and Portland, Maine. Ron's oldest daughter, Jessica, manages the Arlington and Belfast stores. His wife, Mary, and daughter Phoebe, also support the business, although they are not as actively involved.

MOLDING CHARACTER

Monroe Salt Works is the product of Ron's lifetime of pottery pursuits. Trained as an engineer, he followed his calling after college by serving in the Peace Corps in Peru. "Life was very close to the bone there," Ron explains. He returned to the States in 1968 to learn pottery at North Carolina's Penland School of Crafts. In 1971 he moved to Maine, where he set up a pottery studio on a two-hundred-acre farm.

Ten years later a woman at a crafts fair suggested that Ron apply for a pilot project in the Dominican Republic aimed at helping communities become self-sufficient. In just one year, Ron taught thirty-five people how to build kilns, make their own bricks, develop glazes, and ultimately make a living from their pottery.

That success brought him to Paraguay in 1983 to inspire another community of seventy-five potters. There, he built new kilns to make the pottery stronger and set up a school to teach glazing and form. "The people there were afraid to stand out," Ron says. "We tried to help

them express agricultural themes—not to think about high art or museums but to communicate their feelings for what they did on a daily basis."

Back in Maine in 1984, after brief stints as a carpenter and painter, Ron committed himself to his pottery business. He sent some pieces to the 1986 New York Gift Show and was encouraged by the positive response. "People hadn't seen anything like it before," he recalls.

Today his pieces range from $16 for a mug to $220 for a platter, but the prices don't reflect their true value. "I try to make honest pots," Ron says, "pots that don't pretend to be something they're not. They come from the heart."✦

Ally of the Dolls

DOLL MAKER ANNE CHASE SANREGRET USES HER SCULPTING TALENTS IN TWO WONDERFULLY CREATIVE AND GENEROUS WAYS.

Above: Sculptor Anne Chase Sanregret looks over clay faces in various stages of development. Later she'll add makeup and facial hair to them to get the look she wants.

Throw open the cupboards in sculptor Anne Chase Sanregret's tidy studio in the Los Angeles suburb of Diamond Bar, and you'll be dazzled by all the fabrics and trims she's amassed, which she combines to produce her lifelike Old World Santa dolls. One cupboard is neatly filled with fun scraps of all kinds, recycled from vintage coats and garments. Another compartment holds a rainbow of suedes and leathers. Faux furs fill a nearby set of drawers. One-of-a-kind knitted sweaters and fancy fabrics such as lamés and brocades occupy their own separate shelves. And accessories—bells, angels, lanterns, musical instruments, and small animal figures—find a home in another area of the workroom.

Just looking at all the possibilities for robes, trims, and accessories never fails to get Anne's creative juices flowing. She finds it helps that everything is well displayed. "I'm constantly organizing," Anne says. "Every two weeks, I'll take an inventory and reorganize. I say that my work is 40 percent sculpting and sewing and 60 percent organizing."

Written by Allison Engel ✦ *Photographs by Perry Struse*

This "Tibetan Santa," made in 2000, stands
36 inches tall and rides a 27-inch llama.
His sumptuous robe and hat are made from an
antique fabric with beading and embroidery.
"I was terrified to cut into it," Anne says.
The price tag on this doll is $1,500.

Opposite: *The "Snow King Santa" at* left *wears a magnificent alpaca eight-gored coat lined in gold lamé. His beard, like those on the other Santas in the photo, is made from Tibetan goat fur. Anne has electrified her "Snow King Santa" with tiny white lights intertwined with white holly berries on his staff. At* far right *is another thirty-six-inch-tall figure, "Russian Santa," who also carries a lighted staff. In the* center *is the red-coated "Traveling Santa," who comes with a suitcase and a globe. He was made for a woman who loves to travel.*

FIVE DECADES OF DOLLS

Anne has been involved in doll making for more than fifty years, starting when she worked as a teacher on a Navajo reservation and showed Native American children how to make soft dolls. Dolls became an even greater part of her life when she taught special education classes in inner-city Los Angeles during the riots of 1992. In that emotionally draining time, teachers were urged to take up outside hobbies. Anne first helped her students create decorated jars that they sold at Christmastime to earn money to buy family presents.

The following summer, the former fine arts major took a sculpting class. "I decided to make something happy, and Santa seemed the happiest thing around," she recalls. She sold her first Santa doll (along with several others) the first day she exhibited them at a show. She now makes about two dozen dolls a year and has regular collectors who buy from her directly. One faithful fan owns eighteen of her pieces.

Anne's creations sell for hundreds of dollars up to several thousand dollars each and are much more than mere dolls. They exist as dramatic tableaux, complete with supporting animal characters and props. She has electrified some with tiny Christmas lights. Two of her Santas stand in the lobby of a children's hospital in the Philippines. Others stand in the lobbies of prominent hotels and office buildings.

Anne makes some dolls to order, with carefully chosen accessories to honor or memorialize a certain person. The names of her three children and five grandchildren often are used in the titles she gives her creations.

ONLY THE BEST WILL DO

It's easy to see why Anne's dolls are so popular. The faces, fashioned from Super Sculpey modeling clay, are amazingly realistic. It can take her up to eight hours to get a doll's features just right. She then paints the face, using makeup rather than paint, which she admits is unorthodox but produces the results she wants.

This "Santa of the Snows," done in 1999, is a white fleece-robed doll who gently holds a white dove. The trim on his robe is faux fur with gold braid.

Also time-consuming are her searches for exquisite fabrics. Her Santa robes are made from the highest-quality velvets, alpacas, French and Italian silks, and antique beaded and embroidered materials that can cost her more than one hundred dollars a yard. She orders fine Tibetan and Icelandic goat fur for the beards and prowls antique shops for vintage toys and accessories for her Santas to carry. She is very particular about what she buys. "I shop constantly," she says, "but I buy very little."

Above: Anne makes custom Santas to honor or commemorate special people. "A Ship for Dr. Chris" is the name of this nautical Santa, who wears a knitted wool sweater and boating shoes. He was made to honor the memory of a young doctor who loved the sea.

Right: This tableau shows several of Anne's Old World Santas with their reindeer. Her time-consuming details include sculpted feet on the Santas and handmade boots. Even the reindeer have hand-sewn saddles. The Santa at far right ("Walking with Deer") wears a chocolate leather coat trimmed in sheared beaver. The leather came from a coat Anne found in an antique shop. At near right is "Mountain Santa on a Log" surrounded by squirrels, chipmunks, and foxes. In the center is "Galloping Through the Night," a Santa charging through the forest dressed in a fox-fur jacket with matching boots.

Here's Anne at the Speech and Language Development Center in Buena Park, California, one of the many schools, nursing homes, and social service agencies where she teaches sculpting as art therapy.

Anne, whose mother was a "brilliant seamstress," has been sewing since she was twelve. She designs all her own patterns and painstakingly cleans and conditions the heavy fabrics and furs she collects. Sewing with furs already has worn out four sewing machines, she says.

In recent years, she has concentrated on Old World Santas with an alpine theme. Why create alpine dolls in perpetually sunny southern California? one might ask. The answer is simple. Anne grew up in Michigan and says that she enjoys "thinking about mountains, trees, and snow. It brings back good memories for me."

She also likes the idea that her mountain Santas use recycled leather and furs. "I like animals and would never harm one," she says. By reusing the furs and leathers she finds in antique and thrift shops, she feels she's giving them a second life.

THE SPIRIT OF GIVING

Anne has brought sculpting and doll making to her teaching and volunteer work for decades, too. Every month she visits a different volunteer center, teaching Girl Scouts, nursing home residents, abused children, the blind, and others to make their own one-of-a-kind clay Christmas animals. "I've taught troubled children all my life," she says, "and I strongly believe in the power of art therapy." She asks her students to name the Christmas animals they create and then to explain why they chose the accessories they did. She beams as she tells of lethargic nursing home residents becoming animated and engaged while talking about the Christmas mice they just made.

Anne gives classes in her studio regularly, leading eight students at a time in a two-day adventure during which they make their own sculpted Santas. "It's exhilarating," she says of her teaching. In addition to her studio classes, she is a part-time professor of special education at Cal State, Fullerton, where she supervises the work of student teachers. And she takes classes herself, traveling at least once a year to a different noted doll maker around the country to hone her skills. One day she hopes to travel and teach Santa-making from coast to coast.

Being surrounded by Santa year-round is "total happiness," she says. "You get to work with your hands and your mind, and create joy."✦

These clay Christmas animals were made by the students at the Speech and Language Development Center. Students turned lumps of clay into unique Christmas figures, which Anne then fired in her home oven, returning a week later with the finished sculptures.

Chain Saw Carver

THIS OREGON WOOD CARVER WIELDS CHAIN SAWS AND
OTHER POWER TOOLS WITH THE FINESSE OF A SURGEON
TO CREATE MASTERPIECES LARGE AND SMALL.

*Above: With the strawberry fields at his rural
workshop behind him, Richard Nosiglia poses
with his chain saw between a roughed-out Santa
and another Santa ready for painting.*

R ichard Nosiglia carves all sorts of figures, both animal and human, but nothing takes quite as much out of him as his Santas. "I think of Russian icon painters or the Santos carvers in New Mexico, where their work becomes a form of meditation," he says. "Really, Santa is our national saint. It's not like carving a bear, which can be stylized. Making a human representation of Santa is hard work."

FALLING INTO A NEW CAREER

Richard, who lives in Salem, Oregon, with his wife and two sons, comes from a family of artists and holds a bachelor's degree in sculpture. In college, he worked primarily in cast aluminum and bronze, and after graduating, he became a painting contractor. Then a fall from a ladder in 1993 changed his life—and his vocation.

Written by Allison Engel ✦ *Photographs by Perry Struse*

This trio of carved Santas ranges from 24 inches to 36 inches tall. The Santas at center and right are earlier pieces, and the figure at left with the windswept beard is a newer example.

As he recovered from his dramatic 35-foot spill, Richard spent a lot of time reading and dreaming about wood carving. Just before Christmas in 1993, he met noted chain saw carver Steinar Karlsen at a show in Eugene, Oregon, and was so impressed that he asked to become Karlsen's apprentice. For the next six months, Richard spent six hours a day five days a week learning the rudiments of the craft.

Carving figures with a chain saw has a long history that began in America's rough-and-tumble logging camps. Richard respects that tradition but also has an affinity for European art, thanks to his great-grandfather, who was an Italian stone sculptor.

CARVING THE SANTAS

Richard's designs are his own, often inspired by books of clip art or old postcards. But no matter how large or small the project, he roughs out each piece with a chain saw, reserving smaller hand tools for the fine detail. He uses a disc grinder with a sanding wheel to grind the carving marks out of the wood and then, if necessary, a die grinder for the final shaping. A Dremel rotary tool fitted with small carving bits is called upon for the delicate finish work. The bits are so small that they look like dental tools, Richard says. The final steps are sanding, painting, and finishing.

Richard generally produces two sizes of Old World Santas. He calls the smaller, mantel-size figures that are twelve to fourteen inches tall "candlepin Santas" because they remind him of the candlepin bowling pins popular in New England. His larger pieces, often placed in entry-ways or in front of fireplaces, stand 2½ to 3 feet tall.

His Father Christmases are known for their dour expressions. Many sport beards that completely cover their mouths. "Getting them to smile is difficult," Richard admits, "because covering the mouth with the beard is a particular style that I like." The twinkling eyes help to make up for dourness, however.

ATTENTION TO DETAIL

No two of Richard's Santas are ever exactly alike, but all wear sumptuous robes with plenty of ornate detail incised on the inner garments. The richness of the fabric is suggested by decorative designs cut into the wood, and painted gold or a contrasting color. Tiny cuts on the hems and cuffs suggest ermine or other furs.

"Victorians were fond of elaborate patterns, and I try to emulate them," Richard says. He draws his inspiration from sources as varied as Gothic stained-glass windows and Italian holiday pastries. "Actually," he says, "my Santas are a confection of design and intellect. It takes me a long time to work out all the elements of the design, to make it flow and not be cluttered—like a latticework that stands on its own but is light in conception. It's the hardest part of creating a Santa of this type—harder than the physical work of carving."

Richard's favorite Old World Santa to date is this wine-robed beauty. He has an intricately carved inner robe of forest green.

Opposite: *These tall, thin figures are known as "candlepin Santas" because they're reminiscent of the tall bowling pins known as candlepins. Each is about a foot tall and bears a unique facial expression.*

Richard uses many species of wood in his carving, including butternut, walnut, cherry, maple, and myrtle. For his small Santas, he prefers using lodgepole pine, which he harvests himself in a forest near Bend, Oregon. This involves securing a firewood-cutting permit and searching for dead or downed trees. He returns to his studio with a pickup load of timber—enough to last a year. For the large Santas, he uses Port Orford cedar, an indigenous Oregon species. The cedar is "incredibly fragrant," which makes it especially pleasant to use.

Richard markets his Santas to several galleries in Oregon and also sells at crafts shows in the state. The smaller Santas sell for $150 to $175, and the large figures go for about $1,200.

CREATIVE CHALLENGES

When he's not carving Santas and Father Christmases, Richard creates signs, benches, logs, walking sticks, and figures from nature. Commission work brings him such

creative challenges as carving a 650-pound Halloween pumpkin for a farmers' market and various stump sculptures on the sites of downed trees. To date, he has completed nine decorative stumps in designs representing turtles, bears, eagles, and a pirate as well as a 14-foot carving of three bear cubs climbing up a tree. These projects often take a full week to complete and can mean working before an audience of onlookers. Seeing a huge stump waiting to be carved can be daunting, Richard says, but it makes a lot of economic sense. "It's no more expensive to carve a stump than to grind it up!"

REVIVING AN OLD ART

Until twenty years ago, Richard would have characterized wood carving as a dying art. The decline goes back to the beginning of the twentieth century, when wooden ships gave way to metal ships and the demand for figure-head carvers dried up. Later, new sidewalk ordinances banned cigar-store Indians from America's downtowns, and the number of commercial wood carvers declined further still. But in the 1980s, a jump in the number of retired people who were taking up wood carving as a hobby caused interest to surge. Richard credits the current popularity of whittling and wood carving to the fact that they are creative, satisfying, and inexpensive hobbies. Carving is appealing to newcomers, but it's also an unforgiving art. "With metal sculpture, you can always add on," Richard says. "But once wood is cut, it's gone."✦

Above: *Walking sticks are another specialty of Richard's. He often makes them to order.*

Opposite: *A grouping of some of Richard's earliest Santa figures is arranged on his mantel. These Victorian-style Santas stand about six inches tall.*

Familiar Faces

FROM THE WRINKLES ON SANTA'S BROW TO THE BUCKLES ON HIS BOOTS,
BARBARA VAN NOY KNOWS EVERY FACET OF THE JOLLY OLD MAN.

Above: After three to four months spent crafting each Santa, Barbara is ready for them to start spreading their joy. She poses here with "The Gift-Giver," but Barbara herself bears gifts of her own: extraordinary talent, a childlike imagination, and maybe even a little magic.

Opposite: The Toy and Miniature Museum of Kansas City bought "Sshhh, No Fair Peeking!" in the spring of 1999. He's a natural in front of a circa-1860 fairy-tale dollhouse from Lebanon, Pennsylvania.

What do you want your Santa to look like? Barbara VanNoy asked each of her three children that question when she started making Santas in 1996. Fourteen exquisite handmade dolls later, she's still finding new interpretations.

Whether he's clad in a classic cherry-red coat or draped in a rich Victorian velvet gown, each of Barbara's one-of-a-kind Santas embodies the true spirit of Christmas. With their sacks of handmade wishes-come-true and even music boxes that play along, they're all decked out to delight. Besides their flawlessly detailed costumes, Barbara's dolls are distinguished by their expressions. Captivating eyes, seasoned smile lines, and finely detailed teeth make them so lifelike, many people do a double-take when they see them.

Written by Judith Stern Friedman ✦ Photographs by Steve Struse

MAKING MERRY

With each one taking more than four hundred hours spread over two to three months to create, Barbara's two-foot-tall Santas are limited edition works of art. A full-time mom, Barbara creates them in her spare time in the Ozark Hills of Springfield, Missouri, thirty miles north of Branson. Her family—sons Jeff, 28, and Jim, 23; daughter Sarah, 15; and husband John—are her most avid fans as she redefines Santa from her downstairs studio.

Drawing inspiration from antique postcards, books, magazines, and holiday displays, Barbara likes to have all the details in her head before she even starts a doll. "You put little notes away here and there. Then you put them all together," she explains.

The texturing of the skin on the faces and hands is one of Barbara's specialties, and it can take as long as two painstaking weeks to accomplish. Using ProSculpt polymer clay and intricate tools, she creates 2¾-inch faces based on photographs of people in her life. One doll resembles a neighbor; another has her father's features. In addition to realistic nostrils and detailing, each Santa sports his own set of dentures molded from a mix of translucent and white Sculpey clays. Hand-tied eyelashes and dreamy porcelain eyes are the finishing touches that add to the remarkable human likeness.

Once complete, the appendages are attached to a soldered brass frame in a custom-fitted bodysuit. After soft-sculpting muscles and rolls of fat, Barbara sews the undergarments. "Santa always has long johns, socks, and a T-shirt," she says. It's the start of repeated visits to her walk-in closet, which is stuffed with the makings for Santa's suit. "I can spend an entire day looking for just the right fabric," she says.

Barbara prefers to work with vintage fabrics, although she says they're increasingly hard to find. "I try to stick with silks and natural fibers," she adds. Santa's beard is made from natural mohair, which she gets "straight from

Barbara's Victorian Santa, "A Gift for You," fulfills the vision of her middle child, Jim. The china doll, made of ProSculpt polymer clay and antique handkerchiefs, is one of Barbara's handmade toy treasures.

Opposite: *Barbara found her calling in 1996, when her third Santa, "Father Christmas Cares for All," won first place in the Silver Dollar City Doll Challenge in Branson, Missouri.*

the goat." The mohair requires washing, welting, and cleaning, which she does a few strands at a time, before it's applied to Santa's scalp and face. After adding hand-made accessories and a few store-bought toys, Barbara is ready to introduce each newly minted miniature to his adoring fans.

SPECIAL GIFTS

"I'm a do-it-yourself person," Barbara explains. The third oldest of seven children, she grew up making her own doll clothes. Later, majoring in art at Southwest Missouri, she honed her skills. Still, Barbara says experience has always been her best teacher.

Barbara credits her mentor and internationally renowned doll-maker Judith Klawitter whose Santa dolls she first saw in a 1995 issue of *Better Homes and Gardens® Santa Claus®* magazine. "I wanted those Santas for my children," she recalls, "but I realized I couldn't afford three of them. So I bought some clay to try to make them myself."

Barbara hid her first attempt, which she now refers to as "the scary Santa," but she quickly learned from her mistakes. With her third Santa, "Father Christmas

Cares for All" *(on page 118),* she won first place in a national doll competition. Although friends and family continued to encourage her, Barbara still saw much room for improvement.

The fall of 1997 marked the turning point. Barbara took her first workshop with Judith Klawitter, who encouraged her to sell her Santas professionally. In April 1998, Barbara's "Have You Been Good?" Santa was sold within three minutes at the opening of a Doll Arts show in Santa Fe, New Mexico.

Today, Barbara's Santas sell for a minimum of two thousand dollars each and are displayed in museums and galleries nationwide, including the Toy and Miniature Museum of Kansas City. "I had never seen art dolls of such high quality until I visited this museum," Barbara recalls. Now one of her own Santas is part of the museum's collection.

So, which one of Barbara's many Santa creations is her personal favorite? "Each one is my favorite at the time, and then it goes on," she says. In the fall of 1999, she began teaching skin-texturing classes at her home. Meanwhile, she has been experimenting with babies and other figures, but she always keeps returning to Santa. "It's comforting to look at him," she says. Her radiant renditions of this legendary hero spread smiles that are just as magical as the jolly old man himself.✦

Above: *Barbara takes special care with her Santas' beards. After washing, welting, and cleaning natural mohair, she tediously applies the fibers a few strands at a time for a startlingly realistic look.*

Opposite: *"Cookie Break" was Barbara's second Santa, which she created for her oldest son, Jeff. Barbara makes all parts of the dolls herself, except for the bases, which are built by her husband, John.*

If you're reading this book, you probably don't
need to announce your passion to others. Even so,
our "Santa Collector" sign will make it official.

Now that you've seen the
Santas others are collecting and
creating, it's time to do some
Kris Kringle crafting of your own.
Our thorough instructions
will help bring Santa to life
in record time!

PERSONAL EXPRESSIONS

Hooked on Santa

The finished wall hanging is 8×8".

MATERIALS

- **Pattern,** *page 126*
- **Tracing paper**
- **Pencil**
- **Iron-on transfer pen or red-dot transfer paper**
- **Piece of burlap large enough to fit over your rug hoop**
- **Sewing machine**
- **14" freestanding or lap rug-hooking hoop or frame**
- **Rug-hooking cutter with #8 and #4 blades or a rotary cutter and cutting mat**
- **Ruler**
- **¼ yard of gold wool for the background**
- **10×12" piece of red wool for the hat and suit**
- **12×12" piece of black wool for the hat trim, eyes, and border**
- **10×12" piece of white wool for the beard and eyebrows**
- **4×10" piece of tan wool for the hat trim**
- **4×10" piece of flesh-color wool for the face**
- **2×8" piece of light-brown wool for the nose outline**
- **2×8" piece of rose-color wool for the cheeks**
- **8½×8½" piece of black wool for the backing**
- **Coarse or primitive size rug hook**
- **Iron**
- **Towel**
- **Curly wool for the mustache**
- **Piece of white string for attaching the mustache and bell**
- **1 small jingle bell**
- **Tacky glue**
- **Black permanent felt-tip marker**
- **6—14" strands of black yarn**

TRANSFER THE PATTERN

Enlarge the pattern on *page 126* and transfer it onto tracing paper. Then, using an iron-on transfer pen, red-dot transfer paper, or the method of your choice, transfer the design onto the burlap.

PREPARE YOUR MATERIALS

Machine-stitch along the outside border of the pattern, keeping as close to the pattern lines as possible. This will ensure that your hooking won't come loose when you trim away the excess burlap. Also, machine-stitch around the outer edges of the burlap to keep it from fraying. Stretch the burlap over a rug frame or hoop, making sure it's taut.

Using a rug-hooking cutter with a #4 blade, cut all of the wool you'll use for the face (including the eyes, eyebrows, nose, and cheeks) into ⅛"-wide strips. Use a rug-hooking cutter with a #8 blade or a quilter's rotary cutter and cutting mat to cut the rest of the wool, except the black backing square, into ¼"-wide strips. All strips should be between 10" and 14" long.

HOOK THE DESIGN

Start by hooking the outer border, using the black ¼" wool strips to hook one row all the way around. Add one row of hooking inside the border, using the ¼" gold wool strips.

Hook the eyes and the nose area, and then the cheeks, eyebrows, and the remaining areas of the face, using the ⅛" wool strips in the colors indicated *above*.

Referring to the pattern on *page 126* for color placement, hook the beard, hat, and suit using the ¼" wool strips in the colors indicated *above*. Use the ¼" gold wool strips to hook the background until it is filled in completely.

FINISH THE PROJECT

Remove the piece from the rug frame and place it facedown on an ironing board. Cover it with a damp towel and press flat with an iron.

Photograph by Scott Little

Enlarge 125%

Hook one end of a piece of white string under the nose, and bring up the other end two threads below that. Cut a few lengths of curly wool, and gather to make a mustache; then tie it in place using the string. Cut off the ends of the string. Attach a bell to the end of Santa's hat in the same manner.

Using tacky glue, glue the hooked piece to the black wool backing. Weight the project with a heavy object until the glue dries. Then trim the excess backing to within ⅛" of the hooking, right up to the stitching line. If any burlap shows through on the sides, color it with a black marker so that it's less visible.

To make the braided hanger, start by holding all six strands of black yarn with ends even and tie a knot about 4" from the top. Braid the strands, and finish with a knot about 4" from the bottom. The loose strands at each end form tassels. Attach the hanger at the top corners of the hooked piece, stitching through the burlap and wool backing. ✦

Designed by Donna Lovelady

Hooking Basics

If you're new to hooking, Donna Lovelady offers this crash course to help you get started:

1 Always start by hooking the outline of your design; then go back and fill it in. If your design is round, follow the curves. If it's square, work vertically or horizontally. After you've hooked your design, hook a line of background around each design motif to firm up the lines.

2 To begin hooking, insert your hook into the top of the burlap. Hold the wool strip in your other hand under the burlap (Diagram 1).

3 Grasp the wool strip with the hook, and pull the end through the top of the burlap (Diagram 2).

4 Skip two burlap threads, insert your hook into the burlap again, and pull the wool up to form your first loop (Diagram 3). Since it isn't a loose end, you'll form a loop. The width of your wool strip determines the height of the loop; your loop should be as high as the strip is wide. Continue in this manner until the strip is finished. Make nice, even loops without twisting the wool. When you make a new loop, the last hole will automatically tighten—the pressure of the loops against each other holds them in place. As you work, be careful not to cross over previous stitches.

5 When you finish the first wool strip, bring the ends to the top of the burlap and trim them to the same height as the loops (Diagram 4). After you press your piece, these ends will be invisible. You can trim them as you go or all at once when the piece is finished.

6 Begin a new strip in the same hole where you just ended. That way, you'll have the same thickness of wool in each hole. It's not necessary to completely use up each strip of wool. If you need to change colors, just bring the end to the top, trim it, and start a new color strip.

7 When you start a new row of strips, always skip about two threads. This will prevent you from hooking your piece too tightly, which will cause it to roll when you remove it from the frame. Hooking tightly can work to your advantage when you're making a pillow, a doll, or anything else that's stuffed. That's because the stuffing will cause the rows of hooking to spread out a bit; tight loops will prevent too much spreading, keeping the burlap from showing.

8 Turn your piece over frequently to make sure it's smooth and has no loose ends. If you spot problems, correct them before continuing. Catching your mistakes early will save you from having to rip out many loops and repeat your work. Don't worry if you spot gaps in the back. But, if you find an opening in the front, go back and fill it in with new loops.

9 When you've finished hooking the entire project, trim any remaining ends. Then, place your piece facedown with a damp towel on top and steam until flat. For larger pieces, like rugs, you may want to use the steam machine at your local dry cleaner.

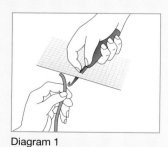

Diagram 1

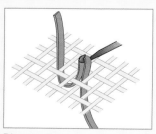

Diagram 2

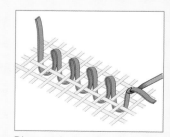

Diagram 3

Diagram 4

Cotton Batting Santas

Finished Santas are about 7 ½" tall.

MATERIALS

For all Santa ornaments:

- **Patterns,** *pages 131–133*
- **Tracing paper**
- **Pencil**
- **Scissors**
- **White cardboard or poster board**
- **Cotton batting (CRF7)**
- **Elmer's Glue-All Multipurpose glue**
- **Small, flat paintbrush**
- **1 yard of $\frac{1}{16}$"-diameter gold cord**

For Santa A:

- **$5\frac{1}{2}$"-long piece of gold Leonian wire-mesh tubing (LT10G)**
- **Old-fashioned Santa face scrap (EF7159)**

- **Dresden trims: Frilly Fleuron Border Gold (DT25G), Fancy Borders Assortment Gold (DT27G), and Button Starlet Gold (DT85G)**
- **Off-white goose-feather sprig (GFS06)**
- **Jack Frost Mica Flakes (HF02)**

For Santa B:

- **Old-fashioned Santa face scrap (A5758)**
- **1 sheet of red tissue paper**
- **$\frac{3}{4}$ yard of $\frac{3}{16}$"-diameter green-and-white-striped cord trim (CRF15)**
- **Dresden trims: Tiny Buttons Gold (DT94G) and Snowflake Paddle Gold (D801G)**

- **Green goose-feather sprig (GFS02)**
- **Icy Flake Diamond Dust (GL4W)**

For Santa C:

- **Old-fashioned Santa face scrap (SQ10)**
- **Dresden trims: Petite Points Border Gold (DT24G), Graduated Stars Gold (DT83G), and Snowflake Paddle Gold (D801G)**
- **Jack Frost Mica Flakes (HF02)**
- **$\frac{3}{4}$ yard of $\frac{1}{4}$"-diameter antique ivory chenille trim (CRF3)**
- **6—3"-long twigs**
- **Floral wire**
- **White acrylic crafts paint**

INSTRUCTIONS FOR ALL SANTAS

Trace the body pattern on *page 131* onto tracing paper and cut out. Use the pattern to trace the body onto poster board; cut out. Trace the pattern onto cotton batting as well, adding an extra ½" on the bottom. Cut out the cotton batting body, and secure to the poster board backing with a small amount of glue. Fold the ½" of excess batting to the back of the poster board, and glue in place to cover the bottom edge.

Transfer the robe pattern onto tracing paper; cut out. Trace the robe pattern onto cotton batting, and cut out the robe.

ASSEMBLING SANTA A

Cut a 5½"-long piece of gold Leonian wire-mesh tubing, and leave it flat. Do not open it up to create a tube. Center the mesh piece over the cotton batting body, with about ½" of the tubing extending past the bottom. Fold this excess tubing to the back, and glue. Adhere the edges of the tubing to the front of the cotton body with a small amount of glue.

Trim the Santa face scrap by cutting away excess paper from around the beard. Do not trim the brown fur hat. Glue the Santa face onto the cotton figure, with the hat at the very top.

Trace the hat pattern, on *page 131* onto tracing paper; cut out. Trace the hat pattern onto cotton batting and cut out. The hat begins as a 3½" triangle. Turn the bottom edge up about ½", and glue to make a brim. Apply glue to the fur hat on the Santa face scrap, then position the cotton batting hat over it, aligning the back of the brim section with the fur hat. Be sure to maintain a nice

Santa A

Santa C

Santa B

Cloaked in fleecy robes of cotton batting adorned with reproduction Victorian paper scraps and Dresden trims, these Santa ornaments have an Old World flair. Mother and daughter team Beatrice Blum Boyce and Diane S. Boyce patterned their designs after holiday decorations popular in the late 1800s.

curve around Santa's face. Fold the ends of the brim to the back of the figure. The hat will meet in a point at the back of the neck, forming a cone shape, as shown in the diagram *below*. Finish by folding the point of the hat to the back of the figure, with the point extending about ½" below the brim, and glue in place.

Center the Santa figure ⅛" up from the bottom of the cotton batting robe. Fold down about ¾" of the rounded top of the robe at the back of the head; refer to the robe pattern for fold placement. Form the collar by wrapping the folded portion of the robe to the front of the figure, with the fold just overlapping the sides of Santa's beard, as shown *below*.

Bring the top outer edges of the robe to the center of the figure, about 4" from the bottom, allowing the excess batting at the center to form folds. Apply a small amount of glue to the edges of the batting, gather, and press onto the figure to form arms.

Fold the robe open at the center, on both sides of the Santa, so the wire-mesh undergarment is visible. Tack each side in place with a small amount of glue at the top and bottom.

Trace the cuff pattern onto tracing paper; cut out. Trace the cuff pattern onto batting, and cut out two cuffs. Fold batting in from the left and right edges to meet in the center on each cuff and secure with a bit of glue. Fold the top and bottom of each cuff to meet in a circle. Glue the backs of the cuffs below the collar, centering them over the gathered arms.

Add trim to the robe by gluing a Dresden star above the cuffs, plus Dresden borders around the robe edges and the brim of the hat. Tuck and glue an off-white goose-feather sprig into Santa's arm. Highlight the robe and hat by applying glue to select areas with a small paintbrush and sprinkling with mica flakes.

For the hanger, cut a 5" length of ¹⁄₁₆" gold cord. Form a loop, and tuck and glue the ends of the cord under the collar at the back of the figure.

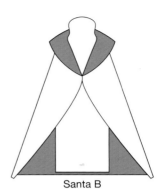

Santa B

ASSEMBLING SANTA B

Trace the robe pattern onto red tissue paper, and cut out. Align the tissue-paper cutout atop the cotton batting robe, applying a small amount of glue around the edges to secure the two pieces. Lay the robe with the tissue paper side up. Center the prepared Santa figure on the robe, placing it ⅛" up from the bottom. Fold about ¾" of the rounded top of the robe to the back of the head. Form the collar by wrapping the folded edge to the front of the body. The collar should meet 2½" from the top of the head. Glue a large Dresden snowflake paddle to the body between the collar lapels. Fit the Santa face scrap onto the body piece, and lightly tack the collar into place around the face scrap with glue.

Bring the top outer edges of the robe to the center of the figure, about 4" from the bottom, allowing the excess batting at the center to form folds. Apply a small amount of glue to the edges of the batting, gather, and press onto the figure to create arms.

Starting at the bottom of the collar, glue the green-and-white-striped decorative cord along the edge of the red tissue all the way around the robe, ending at the bottom of the collar.

Trace sleeve pattern onto tracing paper and cut out. Trace a right and left sleeve onto cotton batting and cut out. To form a

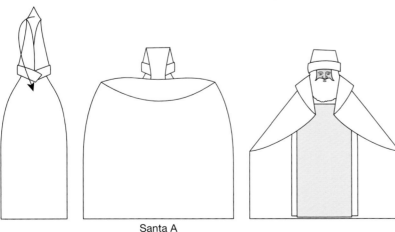

Santa A

sleeve, fold cotton to meet in the center back, and glue down. Cut two 2½×¼" strips of red tissue paper. Glue one onto the edge of each sleeve, forming a cuff. Glue the left sleeve and right sleeve below the collar, with the cuffs meeting at the center.

Trim by gluing Dresden buttons on the underskirt of the batting figure. Tuck and glue a green goose-feather sprig into Santa's arm. Highlight select areas by applying glue with a small paintbrush and sprinkling with icy flake diamond dust.

For the hanger, cut a 5" length of ¹⁄₁₆" gold cord. Form a loop, and tuck and glue the ends of the cord under the collar at the back of the figure.

ASSEMBLING SANTA C

To make the hat, follow the instructions for Santa A, but do not glue the hat brim on the front of the figure because you will later slide the face scrap under the brim.

For the robe, follow the instructions above, but form the arms by tucking leftover bits of cotton batting beneath the robe to add shape to them. Cut the edges of the robe at the hemline to make graceful curves. Edge the collar and robe with chenille roping followed by a row of ¹⁄₁₆"-diameter gold cord. Decorate around the hat, collar, and robe with Dresden border trim; then place four Dresden stars on either side of the robe and a snowflake just above the arms. Use glue sparingly to secure trims.

Carefully glue in antique Santa face, tucking the head under the hat brim and leaving part of the beard resting on top of the collar. Glue the hat brim down, and add

a row of ¹⁄₁₆"-diameter gold cord around the top of the brim.

Make a bundle of small twigs, securing them with floral wire. Dab white paint onto several branches and sprinkle with mica flakes. Let the paint dry; then tuck and glue the bundle under one arm of the figure. Highlight the robe and hat by applying glue to select areas with a small paintbrush and sprinkling with mica flakes.

For the hanger, cut a 5" length of ¹⁄₁₆" gold cord. Form a loop, and tuck and glue the ends of the cord under the collar at the back of the figure.✦

*Designed by Beatrice Blum Boyce
and Diane S. Boyce*

Cotton Batting Santa
Body
Cut 1 each

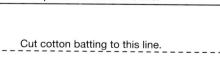

Cotton Batting Santa
Hat
Cut 1 each
Santas A and C

Cut poster board to this line.

Cut cotton batting to this line.

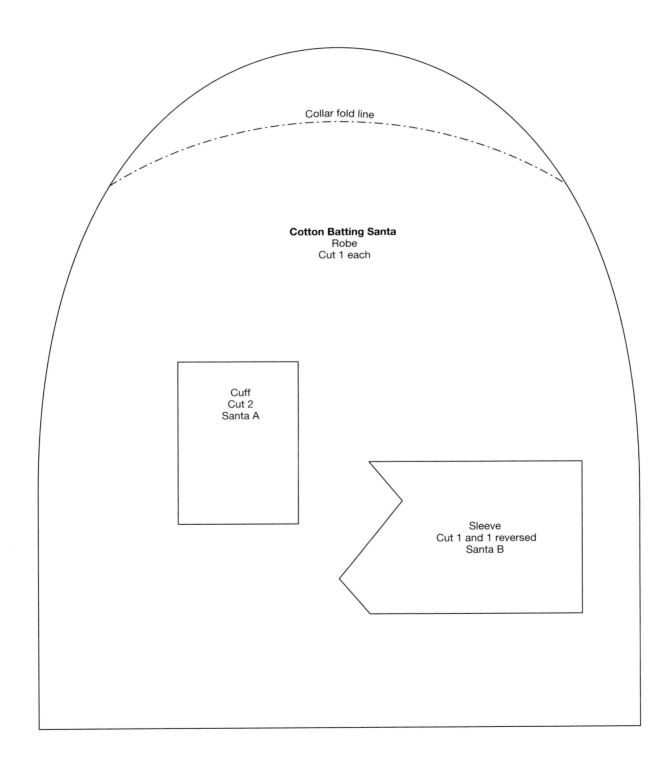

Collar fold line

Cotton Batting Santa
Robe
Cut 1 each

Cuff
Cut 2
Santa A

Sleeve
Cut 1 and 1 reversed
Santa B

Santa Ornament Trio

To round out this charming trio, Wendy Mosbacher teamed
a red Santa Claus and green St. Nick with a beguiling blue
Kris Kringle. Each Santa's personality is reflected in the eye
and hat color, mustache style, and beaded hat trim.

Santa Ornament Trio

Each ornament is approximately 2×4⅜".

MATERIALS

For each ornament:

- Patterns, *page 135*
- 4×7 piece of 28-count Lugana fabric
- Cotton embroidery floss as listed in the keys on *pages 135–137*
- White Caron Kit Kin thread
- Iron
- Hand mixer
- Scissors
- 4×7" piece of coordinating cotton-print backing fabric
- Matching thread
- Sewing machine
- Fiberfill stuffing
- Beading needle
- 1"-wide piece of cardboard
- Toothbrush

For Kris Kringle (blue):

- Mill Hill beads: 4 small white bugle beads (70479), 4 medium white bugle beads (80479), 17 royal pearl seed beads (03021)
- Sewing thread to match bead color
- Blue metallic embroidery floss for the hanger
- Kreinik Pearl (032) Blending Filament for the tassel

For Old St. Nick (green):

- Mill Hill beads: 60 rich red seed beads (03049), 24 creme de mint seed beads (02020), and 4 gold magnifica seed beads (10076)
- Sewing thread to match bead colors
- Kreinik Very Fine #4 gold braid for the tassel

For Santa Claus (red):

- Mill Hill beads: 22 royal pearl seed beads (03021), 2 medium creme de mint bugle beads (82020), 4 small creme de mint bugle beads (72020), and 3 rich red seed beads (03049)
- Sewing thread to match bead colors
- Red metallic embroidery floss for the hanger
- Ecru cotton embroidery floss for the tassel

GENERAL INSTRUCTIONS

Center and stitch the desired face design from the chart on the lugana fabric. Use three plies of floss to work the stitches over two threads of the fabric unless otherwise specified. When stitching the beard, mustache, and eyebrows, use two plies of Kit Kin thread with one ply of white floss.

When you are finished with all of the stitching, place the stitchery facedown on a soft towel, and press from the back.

ASSEMBLE ORNAMENT

To create twisted cording for the hanger, take a 3' length of two plies of floss that matches the hat color, fold it in half, and loop it over a stationary object, like a cabinet knob. Tie the loose ends to the beaters of a hand mixer, and turn on the mixer to twist and tighten the cord. You will need approximately 6" of cording for each hanger. Tie off ends at proper length, and trim excess.

Place stitchery and backing fabric right sides together, laying the hanger in place at the top of the ornament. Machine-stitch along the edge of the stitchery, catching the hanger in the stitching and leaving an opening at the bottom for turning and stuffing. Clip excess fabric to within ¼" of stitching line, turn right side out, and stuff firmly with fiberfill.

Following the bead placement patterns, on *pages 135–137*, attach the beads using one ply of matching thread. For the Old St. Nick ornament, couch the ends of the beaded flower petals and leaves with a matching thread.

Create tassels by wrapping enough plies of floss around a 1" piece of cardboard to get the number of plies for each ornament, listed on *pages 135–137*. Carefully slide the wrapped floss from the cardboard, and tie off about ¼" from one end. Cut the threads on the other end, and shape the tassel before attaching it to the left side of the hat brim with matching floss. Fluff the beard by brushing lightly with a toothbrush.✦

Designed by Wendy Mosbacher

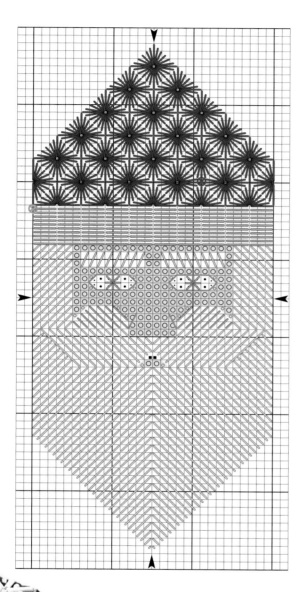

Kris Kringle (Blue)

CROSS-STITCH

ANCHOR		DMC
002	•	000 White (2X)
403	■	310 Black (3X)
1010	◎	951 Ivory (3X)

BACKSTITCH (1X)

1013 ╱ 3778 True terra-cotta – eyes and nose

ALGERIAN EYELET (3X)

1088 ✳ 3790 Beige-gray – eyes

BLENDED NEEDLE ALGERIAN EYELET

137 ✴ 824 Bright blue (1X) and 5291 Metallic royal blue (2X) – hat

SATIN STITCH

868 ╱ 3779 Pale terra-cotta (3X) – cheeks

BLENDED NEEDLE SATIN STITCH

╱ Y1 Caron Kit Kin white thread (2X) and
002 000 White (1X) – eyebrows, mustache, beard, and hair
002 ═══ 000 White (3X) and 032 Kreinik Pearl blending filament (4X) – hatband

TASSEL PLACEMENT (96X)

002 ⊗ 000 White (48X) and Kreinik Pearl blending filament (48X) – hatband

BEAD PLACEMENT (see diagram)

⊗ 03021 Royal pearl seed beads
70479 White small bugle beads
80479 White medium bugle beads

Stitch count: *66 high x 30 wide*

Finished design size:
28-count fabric – 4⅝ x 2⅛ inches

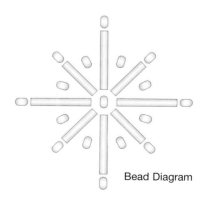

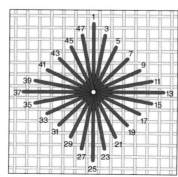

Algerian Eyelet

Bead Diagram

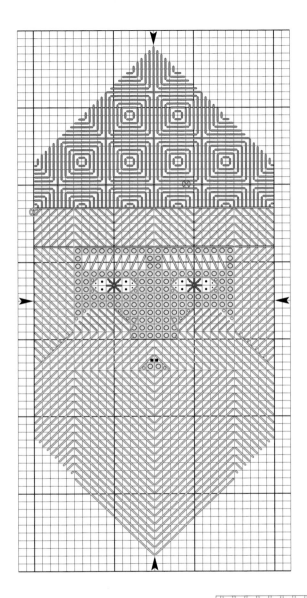

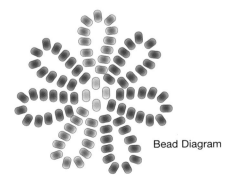

CROSS-STITCH

ANCHOR		DMC	
002	·	000	White (2X)
403	■	310	Black (3X)
1010	◎	951	Ivory (3X)

BACKSTITCH (1X)

1013	╱	3778 True terra-cotta – eyes and nose

ALGERIAN EYELET (3X)

137	✳	824 Bright blue – eyes

SATIN STITCH

002	╱	000 White (3X) – hatband
868	╱	3779 Pale terra-cotta (3X) – cheeks

BLENDED NEEDLE SATIN STITCH

	╱	Y1 Caron Kit Kin white thread (2X) and
002		000 White (1X) – eyebrows, mustache, beard, and hair

BLENDED NEEDLE STRAIGHT STITCH

228	▥	910 Emerald (1X) and 5269 Metallic green (2X) – hat

STRAIGHT STITCH (1X)

▬	002 Kreinik Gold #4 very fine braid – above and below hatband

TASSEL PLACEMENT (48X)

⊗	002 Kreinik Gold #4 very fine braid

BEAD PLACEMENT (see diagram)

⊗	02020 Creme de mint seed beads
	03049 Rich red seed beads
	10076 Gold magnifica seed beads

Stitch count: *66 high x 30 wide*

Finished design size:
28-count fabric – 4⅝ x 2⅛ inches

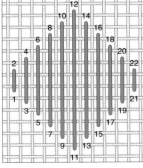

Satin Stitch

Bead Diagram

Bead Diagram

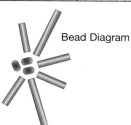

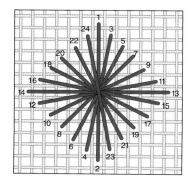

Rhodes Stitch

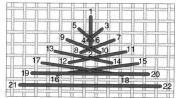

Fishbone Stitch

Santa Claus (Red)

CROSS-STITCH

ANCHOR		DMC	
002	•	000	White (2X)
403	■	310	Black (3X)
1010	◎	951	Blush (3X)

BACKSTITCH (1X)

1013 ╱ 3778 Terra-cotta – eyes and nose

ALGERIAN EYELET (3X)

228 ✳ 910 Emerald – eyes

BLENDED NEEDLE RHODES STITCH

1005 ✸ 816 Garnet (1X) and 5270 Metallic red (2X) – hat

BLENDED NEEDLE FISHBONE STITCH VARIATION

1005 ▲ 816 Garnet (1X) and Metallic red (2X) – hat border

SATIN STITCH

868 ╱ 3779 Rosewood (3X) – cheeks

BLENDED NEEDLE SATIN STITCH

╱ Y1 Caron Kit Kin white thread (2X) and
002   000 White (1X) – eyebrows, beard, and hair

SMYRNA CROSS-STITCH (3X)

002 ✳ 000 White – hat band

STRAIGHT STITCH (3X)

590 — 712 Cream – between face and hat band

— 5270 Metallic red – between hat and hat band

BLENDED NEEDLE STRAIGHT STITCH

🖌 Y1 Caron Kit Kin white thread (2X) and
002   000 White (1X) – mustache

MILL HILL BEADS

● 03021 Royal pearl – hat band

TASSEL PLACEMENT (96X)

590 ⊗ 712 Cream

BEAD PLACEMENT (see diagram)

⊗ 03049 Rich red

72020 Creme de mint small bugle bead

82020 Creme de mint medium bugle bead

Stitch count: *66 high x 30 wide*

Finished design size:
28-count fabric – 4⅝ x 2⅛ inches

Elegant
Father Christmas Doll

The finished Santa is 20" tall.

MATERIALS

- **Patterns,** *page 141*
- **Graph paper**
- **Water-soluble fabric marking pen**
- **⅓ yard of muslin**
- **¾ yard of cream-and-gold star-print fabric**
- **¾ yard of sheer cream fabric**
- **¼ yard of gold satin fabric**
- **¼ yard of blue-and-cream print fabric**
- **Matching sewing threads**
- **Polyester fiberfill**
- **Plastic doll-stuffing pellets**
- **Medium-weight gold twisted cord**
- **Purchased 3¾" porcelain Santa doll head and hands**
- **2½ yards of ⅝"-wide gold-edged cream sheer ribbon**
- **2"-long gold tassel**
- **3—¼"-diameter pearl shank-style buttons**
- **1½ yards of ⅛"-diameter gold twisted cord**
- **Scraps of cream tulle**
- **Potpourri with gold pinecones**
- **Purchased 3"-diameter gold beaded wreath**
- **20" length of ⅜"-wide gold ribbon**

GENERAL INSTRUCTIONS

The overcoat, undercoat, and hood patterns all include ¼" seam allowances. The pattern outline for the leg is the sewing line. Sew all pieces with right sides facing, using ¼" seam allowances unless otherwise directed.

CUT THE FABRICS

Enlarge the patterns on *page 141* onto graph paper. Cut out the pattern pieces.

From the muslin, cut a 16×9" rectangle for the legs, a 10×8" rectangle for the body, and a 16×3¼" strip for the arms. From the star-print fabric, cut one undercoat and one hood. From the sheer fabric, cut one overcoat and one hood. To cut the undercoat and overcoat, first fold each piece of fabric in half lengthwise and then widthwise. From the gold satin fabric, cut a 16×6" rectangle for the boots, two 11×7" rectangles for the bag, and one hood. From the blue-and-cream print fabric, cut two 6½×14" rectangles for the pants.

SEW THE DOLL

For the body, fold the 10×8" muslin rectangle in half so you have a 5×8" rectangle. Sew the 8" edges together for the center back; press the seam allowance open. To form the casing, turn the top edge under ½" and press. Sew ⅜" from the pressed edge, leaving a small opening at the seam. Insert a 12" length of medium-weight cord in the casing.

Sew the 16×6" piece of gold satin to the 16×9" piece of muslin along a 16" edge. Fold the leg/boot fabric in half, right sides together, matching the seam; pin in several places. Use the water-soluble fabric marking pen to trace two legs onto the fabric, placing the boot line at the seam. Sew on the traced lines, leaving the top open. Cut out the legs ¼" beyond the sewn lines; clip the curves and turn right side out. Stuff the legs to the knees with polyester fiberfill. Sew across the knees. Then stuff the legs above the knees and sew the openings closed.

Pin the legs centered in the bottom body opening; sew the opening closed, catching the legs firmly in the stitching. Fill the bottom third of the body with plastic pellets, then firmly stuff the rest of the body with fiberfill. Place the head in the top body opening, and pull the cord ends to gather the fabric tightly around the neck. Add more fiberfill as needed to support the head, and knot the cord.

For the arms, fold the 16×3¼" muslin strip in half widthwise. Sew the long edges together, forming a tube. Turn right side out,

Robed in sheer fabric that's adorned with sentiments of the season, Rhonda Matus's Father Christmas doll is the essence of elegance. Details like pearl buttons, gold cord, a beaded wreath and a satin bag stuffed with potpourri add to the luxe look.

and press, turning under ½" at each end. Hand-sew gathering stitches near the open edges. Tack the center of the arm tube to the upper center back of the body. Stuff each arm with fiberfill. Insert the hands in the openings, and pull the threads to gather the fabric tightly around the groove near the open end of each hand. Tack the arms to the sides of the body to create shoulders.

DRESS THE DOLL

Referring to the pattern *opposite*, sew together the two 6½×14" pieces of blue-and-cream fabric along the 14" sides with the right sides together. Find the center of one 6½" side, and draw a line extending 9" into the fabric. Sew ¼" around the drawn line to form the inseam; cut on the drawn line. Turn the pants right side out. Press the bottom of each leg under ¼" for hems; sew ⅛" from the pressed edges. Press under ½" at the top opening, and hand-sew gathering stitches ¼" from the waist edge. Pull the pants on the doll, and pull the threads to fit the pants snugly around the waist; knot.

Fold the undercoat with right sides together; sew the underarm and side seams. Cut the undercoat along the center line on the front only, and slit the neck opening as shown on the pattern. Turn the undercoat right side out. Press under ½" on the bottom and sleeve edges, and sew ¼" from the pressed edges.

Fold the overcoat with right sides together; sew the underarm and side seams. Cut the overcoat along the center line on the front only, and slit the neck opening as shown on the pattern. Turn the overcoat right side out. To hem, press ½" to the right side of the overcoat at the bottom and sleeve edges. Sew the ⅝"-wide ribbon to the bottom of the sleeves and coat, covering the raw edges.

Machine-baste the neck edges of the overcoat. Slip the overcoat on the undercoat. Pull the basting threads to fit the neck of the overcoat to the undercoat; baste in place. Zigzag-stitch together the center front edges of the coat. Press under ¼" at the center front edges. Sew the ⅝"-wide ribbon along each center front edge.

Place the sheer hood over the star-print hood; treat the two layers as one piece of fabric. Sew the center back seam, catching the 2" gold tassel in the stitching at the tip of the hood. Sew the center back seam of the gold satin hood. With the right side of the satin hood facing the sheer/print hood, sew the front edges together. Turn the hood

right side out and press. Sew ⅝"-wide ribbon along the front edge. Sew the hood to the neck edge of the coat.

Place the coat on the doll. To draw the hood around the neck, wrap medium-weight cord around the neck, and knot tightly, burying the cording.

FINISH THE DOLL

Sew the center front edges of the coat together above the waist with three evenly spaced pearl buttons. For the belt, cut a 28" length of ⅛"-diameter gold twisted cord; knot each end. Wrap the belt around the waist, and tie into a bow.

With right sides together, fold an 11×7" gold satin rectangle in half to measure 5½×7". Sew the side and bottom seams, leaving a ½" opening in the side 1" below the top edge for the drawstring. Turn the bag right side out. For the lining, fold the second gold satin rectangle in half, and sew the side and bottom seams, leaving a 3" opening in the side for turning. Slip the bag inside the lining; sew the top edges together. Turn the bag right side out through the opening in the lining. Sew the opening closed; press. To make the casing, sew a row of stitching ¾" and 1¼" from the top edge of the bag. Insert a 24" length of ⅛"-diameter gold twisted cording through the casing; knot the ends together. Line the bag with tulle scraps, and fill with potpourri.

Tie the 20" length of ⅜"-wide gold ribbon in a bow around the beaded wreath. Place the wreath and potpourri bag on the doll where desired.✦

Designed by Rhonda Matus

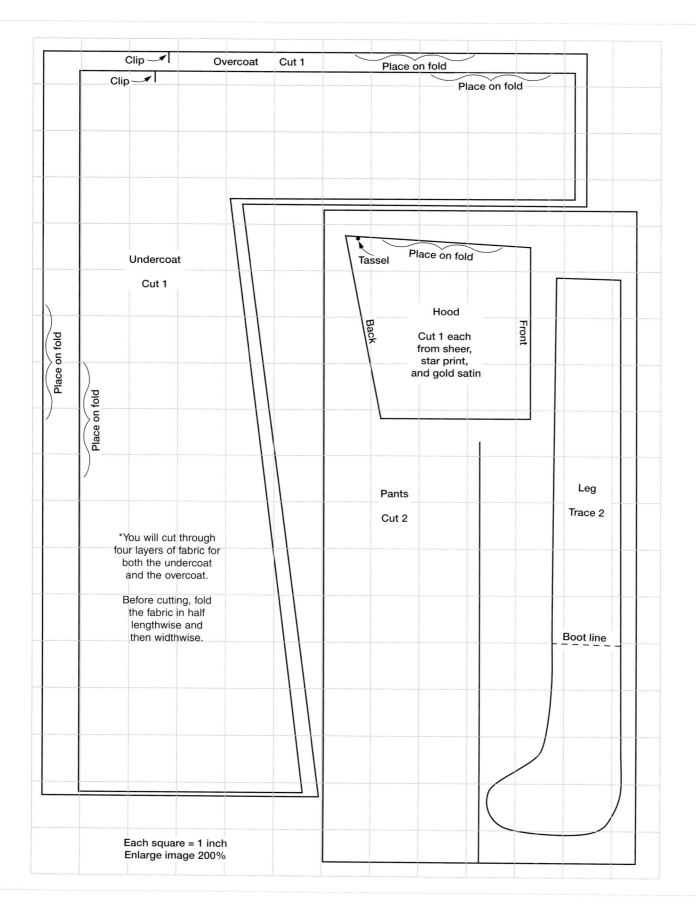

Clip

Overcoat   Cut 1

Place on fold

Clip

Place on fold

Undercoat

Cut 1

Place on fold

Place on fold

Tassel

Place on fold

Hood

Cut 1 each
from sheer,
star print,
and gold satin

Back

Front

Pants

Cut 2

Leg

Trace 2

Boot line

*You will cut through
four layers of fabric for
both the undercoat
and the overcoat.

Before cutting, fold
the fabric in half
lengthwise and
then widthwise.

Each square = 1 inch
Enlarge image 200%

Sign *of the* Times

The finished sign is 14×6".

MATERIALS

- **Pattern, *pages 144–145***
- **14×6×¾" pine "Innkeeper Sign" No. 14071W from Walnut Hollow**
- **100- and 150-grit sandpaper**
- **Tack cloth**
- **Brushes: ¾" flat; ¼" flat; and #000, #0, and #5 round**
- **Delta Ceramcoat Acrylic Colors: Oyster White (OW) 2492, Autumn Brown (AB) 2055, Black (BL) 2506, Santa's Flesh (SF) 2472, Straw (ST) 2078, Mendocino Red (MR) 2406, Tomato Spice (TS) 2098, Medium Foliage Green (MF) 2536, Dark Forest Green (DF) 2096, Wedgwood Blue (WB) 2069, and Gleams Metallic Gold (MG) 2600**
- **Saral red transfer paper or white graphite paper**
- **Stylus**
- **Krylon 1311 Matte-Finish Spray**
- **Pens: Black Ultra Fine Tip Sharpie permanent marker, Black Sakura 01 Pigma Micron Marker, Gold Y&C Gel Pen, and ZIG gold calligraphy paint pen**
- **Kneaded eraser**

PREPARE THE WOOD

Sand the front and edges of the sign with 100- and then 150-grit sandpaper. Wipe with a tack cloth. Do not apply sealer or primer.

PAINT THE BACKGROUND

Using the ¾" flat brush, base-coat the top 4" of the sign front DF. Paint the remaining 1" of the sign front OW. Wipe excess paint out of the brush, but don't moisten the bristles with water. Use the brush to stipple back and forth between the green and white until they blend together, allowing the stipple marks to show. If necessary, add more color until you achieve the desired effect. If the paint begins to dry before you're finished, add a very small amount of water to the brush and complete the blending. Let the paint dry.

TRANSFER THE DESIGN

Using the red transfer paper and a sharp stylus, carefully transfer the pattern on *pages 144–145* to the sign, following the pattern lines precisely. After you've transferred the design, spray the surface with Krylon 1311 Matte-Finish Spray. This allows you to trace over the design lines with the permanent marker, which otherwise would be repelled by the red transfer material.

If you transfer the design using white graphite paper, your lines will be more difficult to see, but you won't need to apply the sealer before tracing with marker.

Trace over the design using the Sharpie permanent marker, again being careful to stay exactly on the pattern lines.

Proclaim your passion for all things Claus with an endearing handpainted plaque depicting Santa about to deliver a pack full of Christmas joys. Designer Jean Wilson created this sign, with crisp lines and gleaming details, to accent an arrangement of Santa collectibles.

Photograph by Scott Little

PAINT THE DESIGN

Paint the design following the pattern *below*. Use round brushes, matching the size of the brush to the size of the design element.

For the holly leaves, berries, chimney, snow, and Santa, use undiluted paints applied in thin layers to achieve maximum coverage. Paint the holly leaves MF, the berries and chimney bricks TS, Santa's face SF, and Santa's suit, hat, and mittens MR. Paint Santa's beard, hair, fur trim, and snow with OW, dabbing on layers of paint to achieve a textured look. Paint Santa's belt BL. Add veins to the holly leaves with AB.

For the toys, dilute the colors with water (using one part paint and one part water) so that some of the background shows through. If you don't achieve sufficient coverage with one coat, let the area dry and apply a second coat. It's better to build the color with several thin layers than a single thick one. Paint the rocking horse OW, using WB and ST for the saddle and AB for the mane, tail, and rocker. Paint the ball using WB, ST, and TS. Paint the bear using ST, with MR for the bow. For the elephant, blend a bit of BL and OW into some WB to create gray. Paint the gifts and bows in various combinations with OW, MR, DF, and ST. Paint the soldier's hat and pants with WB, shirt with MR, accents with ST, and face with SF. Paint the checkerboard with DF and MR. Paint the drum cylinder with WB, rim with MR, and top and trim with ST.

For the inside and outside of Santa's bag, use AB paint diluted to a very thin wash. Keep the brush moving so that the paint doesn't dry too quickly and leave an edge.

To avoid getting color where you don't want it, don't try to push paint into small areas of the design. Instead, always keep the point of the brush aimed at the smaller area and pull the paint out into the larger area. Keep only a very small amount of paint on your brush.

Your goal is to paint into the black design lines, leaving just the thinnest sliver of an outline to define the area. If you make a mistake and paint completely over a line, wait until the paint dries and touch up the line with the Pigma marker. Also use the Pigma marker to draw the fine details such as the eyes and noses on the toys, Santa, and Santa's eyebrows.

PAINT THE EDGES

Using a ¼" brush, paint the topmost routed section ST. Next, paint the lower routed section TS. Let the paint dry, and then paint over the ST with MG. Finally, add a second coat of TS to the lower section.

ADD THE GOLD OUTLINING

Using the calligraphy paint pen, add the gold outlines to the letters in the word "SANTA." Turn the board as you work so that you're always painting just underneath the black outline. Always use the narrow edge of the pen's chisel tip so the lines are of consistent width. For portions of letters where the two outlines are very close together, such as the first leg of the A, fill in with a third stroke.

Use the gold gel pen to add gold outlines to the letters in "COLLECTOR." Once again, reposition the board as you go so that you're always painting underneath the black outline. Also use the gel pen to fill in

the stars and Santa's belt buckle. Because ink from gel pens tends to smear, draw these design elements last, and try to keep your hands from resting on the sign. If some of the ink happens to smear, use a kneaded eraser to remove it while it is still wet and then redraw the line.

Let the ink dry, and then spray the sign with three coats of Krylon 1311 Matte-Finish Spray, allowing ample drying time between coats.✦

Designed by Jean Wilson

Cross-Stitch
Stand-Up Santas

Photograph by Scott Little

Each doll is approximately 5×3×1⅝".

MATERIALS

For each doll:

- **Chart and key,** *pages 148-149*
- **9×10" rectangle of 14-count parchment Aida cloth**
- **Cotton embroidery floss in the colors listed in the key on** *page 148*
- **Iron**
- **Tracing paper**
- **6" square of fusible interfacing**
- **Erasable fabric marker**
- **¼ yard of coordinating cotton fabric**
- **Matching sewing threads**
- **Sewing machine with zipper foot**
- **½ yard of purchased sew-in piping to coordinate with stitchery**
- **2×3" rectangle of medium-weight cardboard**
- **Crafts glue**
- **Polyester fiberfill**

STITCH THE DESIGN

Center and stitch the desired Santa on the Aida cloth. Use three plies of floss to work the stitches over one square unless otherwise specified. Press the finished stitchery facedown.

SEW THE DOLL

Trace the body and base patterns on *page 148*; cut out each pattern.

Center and fuse the interfacing to the back of the stitchery following the manufacturer's instructions. Center the body pattern over the stitchery, and use the erasable fabric marker to draw the shape onto the stitched piece. Cut out ½" beyond the drawn line.

Use the stitched piece as a pattern to cut a matching back from the cotton fabric. Use a zipper foot to baste the piping around the side and top edges of the doll front with the raw edges even.

With right sides together and using the zipper foot, sew the doll front to the back along the basting lines, leaving the bottom edge open. Trim the seams, clip the curves, and turn right side out.

Trace the base pattern on the cardboard, and cut it out. Draw around the cardboard oval on the cotton fabric. Cut out ½" beyond the traced line. Center and glue the cardboard to the back of the cotton fabric. Fold the raw edges to the back, and glue. Let the glue dry.

Stuff the body firmly with fiberfill. Fold the bottom edge of the body under ½". Hand-stitch the base to the bottom of the body.✦

A mystical wanderer robed in blue and violet, a flag-waving patriot toting drum and bugle, and a traditionally garbed figure bearing a pack of gifts—these delightfully detailed cross-stitch dolls depict just a few of the many incarnations of Santa. Stitch one or all three to display in your home or to present to a special collector.

Anchor		DMC	
002	⊡	000	White
110	▲	208	Dark lavender
109	☆	209	Medium lavender
236	◇	317	Pewter
400	⊞	414	Dark steel
370	☒	434	Chestnut
1045	♡	436	Tan
1005	♥	498	Christmas red
683	●	500	Blue-green
208	≡	563	True seafoam
889	◆	610	Deep drab brown
898	✱	611	Dark drab brown
874	▯	676	Light old gold
890	◉	680	Dark old gold
295	✕	726	Topaz
303	∧	742	Tangerine
1022	▢	760	True salmon
133	⊕	796	Medium royal blue
132	⑤	797	Light royal blue
137	✦	798	Delft blue
358	△	801	Coffee brown
045	◙	814	Garnet
882	∟	945	Ivory
360	◪	3031	Mocha
292	⊟	3078	Lemon
144	▥	3325	Medium baby blue
1024	∼	3328	Dark salmon
382	◼	3371	Black-brown
1023	◨	3712	Medium salmon
1008	⊠	3773	Rose-beige

BLENDED NEEDLE

002	⊿	000	White (2X) and
		032	Kreinik Pearl Blending Filament (3X)
398	◘	415	Pearl gray (2X) and
235		318	Light steel (1X)
210	▽	562	Medium seafoam (2X) and
212		561	Dark seafoam (1X)
874	⊖	676	Light old gold (1X) and
		002HL	Kreinik Gold Hi Lustre Blending Filament (3X)
140	★	3755	Dark baby blue (2X) and
977		334	Deep baby blue

BACKSTITCH

236	╱	317	Pewter – Santa A's stockings (1X)
132	╱	797	Light royal blue – Santa A's drum and Santa C's moons (2X)
382	╱	3371	Black-brown – all other stitches (1X)

FRENCH KNOTS

002	○	000	White – Santa A's flag and Santa C's hat (3X wrapped once)
382	●	3371	Black-brown – Eyes of Santa B's doll (2X wrapped once), Santas' eyes, Santa A's knickers buttons, Santa B's buttons, teddy bear's eyes, and boat portholes, (2X wrapped twice)

COUCHING

	╱	5982	Kreinik Forest Green #16 medium braid
268		3345	Medium hunter green (couch with 1X) – Santa B's jump rope
	╱	002HL	Kreinik Gold Hi Lustre #8 fine braid with
		002HL	Kreinik Gold Hi Lustre Blending Filament (1X) – Santa B's wreath ribbon

Santa A stitch count:
60 high x 35 wide

Santa A finished design sizes:
14-count fabric – 4¼ x 2½ inches

Santa B stitch count:
60 high x 37 wide

Santa B finished design sizes:
14-count fabric – 4¼ x 2¾ inches

Santa C stitch count:
60 high x 31 wide

Santa C finished design sizes:
14-count fabric – 4¼ x 2¼ inches

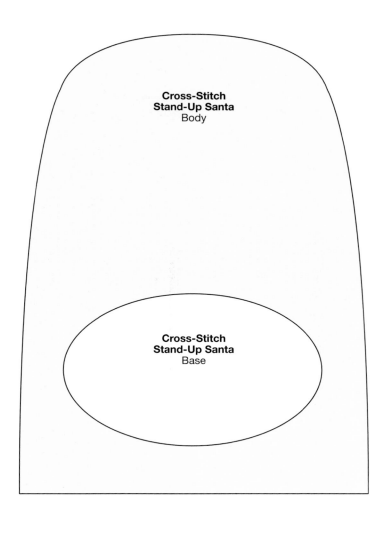

**Cross-Stitch
Stand-Up Santa**
Body

**Cross-Stitch
Stand-Up Santa**
Base

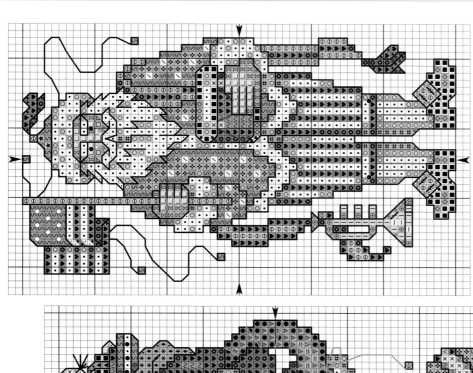

Santa A

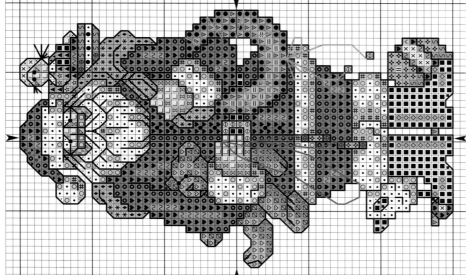

Santa B

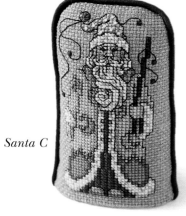

Santa C

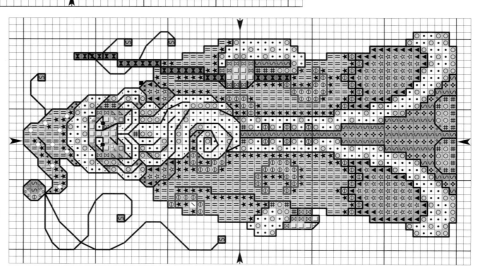

SWEET SENSATIONS

Santa and his elves
make scrumptious appearances
on the pages that follow.
Cleverly disguised as cookies
and cakes, they're fun to make
and a joy to watch disappear.

*A trayful of Santa and elf cookies
in various shapes, sizes, and flavors
will bring smiles all around.*

Photograph by Scott Little

Sweet Santas

SANTA IS DEFINITELY THE STAR OF THE SEASON ON THESE MINI-CAKES. USE THESE PHOTOS AS A GUIDE FOR DECORATING—OR JUST USE YOUR IMAGINATION!

SANTA STAR CAKES

You also can make these stars with the Santa Cutouts cookie dough (see recipe, page 154). Cut with a star-shaped cutter.

Cake mix, any flavor
3   recipes Snow Frosting
       (see recipe, *page 155*)
Paste food coloring, red and green
Small decorating candies

Grease and flour a pan with six 4½-inch star shapes; set aside. Prepare cake mix according to package directions. Pour ⅓ cup batter into each star (reserve remaining batter for another use). Bake in a 350° oven 10 to 12 minutes or until a toothpick comes out clean. Cool in pan on wire rack for 10 minutes. Remove from pan; cool completely on rack.

Divide Snow Frosting into thirds. Color one-third of frosting with red food coloring, one-third with green coloring, and leave one-third white. Spread desired frosting on sides of cakes. Fill each of three pastry bags fitted with medium star tips with a portion of frosting. Decorate as *below*. **Makes six 4½-inch cakes.**

FOR SANTA IN RED SUIT:

Holding the bag vertically, pipe red frosting in small adjoining stars over the cake, except for the face area, tips of four points, and all of fifth point. Pipe a band of red frosting stars across center of fifth point for hat. Using white frosting, pipe beard, hatband, pom-pom on hat, boots, and gloves. For nose and eyes, attach decorating candies

with a little frosting. Use decorating candies for buttons. Let dry until set.

FOR SANTA'S ELF:

Prepare as for Santa in Red Suit, *except* use green frosting. Color some of the frosting a darker shade of green and use for hat, boots, and gloves. Pipe on beard. Attach candies as shown *above*. Let dry until set.

FOR SANTA IN STRIPED SUIT:

Frost top of cake with white frosting. Holding the bags at a 45° angle, pipe red and green stripes over the cake, *except* for face and hat. Pipe stripes of red frosting for hat. Using red or green frosting, pipe hatband, pom-pom on hat, gloves, and boots. Pipe beard and attach candies as *above*. Let dry until set.

Written by Sandra J. Mosley ◆ Food styling by Dianna Nolin ◆ Photographs by Scott Little

These roly-poly Santa Stars are sure to steal the show.

Diamond
Santa

SANTA CUTOUTS

This sugar cookie dough is the base for Diamond Santas and Elves, Santa-in-the-Moon Cookies, and Jolly Santas.

⅓ cup butter (no substitutes)
⅓ cup shortening
¾ cup granulated sugar
1 teaspoon baking powder
  Dash salt
1 egg
1 tablespoon milk
1 teaspoon vanilla
2 cups all-purpose flour

Beat butter and shortening in a large bowl with an electric mixer on medium to high speed for 30 seconds. Add sugar, baking powder, and salt; beat until combined. Beat in egg, milk, and vanilla. Beat in as much of the flour as you can with the mixer. Stir in remaining flour with a wooden spoon. Cover dough and chill about 3 hours or until easy to handle.

Roll dough on a lightly floured surface to ⅛-inch thickness. Cut as desired. Place shapes 1 inch apart on an ungreased cookie sheet.

Bake in a 375° oven for 7 to 8 minutes or until the bottoms are lightly browned. Cool 1 minute on cookie sheet. Transfer cookies to wire racks; cool completely.

DIAMOND SANTAS AND ELVES

Delight children with these winking Santas and sparkling elves.

Santa Cutouts dough
  (see recipe, *at left*)
Powdered Sugar Icing
  (see recipe, *page 157*)
Paste food coloring, red
  and/or green
Nonpareils, flaked coconut, small
  decorating candies, green-
  colored sugar, and crystal sugar
  or granulated sugar

Diamond
Elf

Roll dough on a lightly floured surface to ⅛-inch thickness. Cut into diamonds with a 2½- to 3½-inch cookie cutter or make your own diamond pattern. Place 1 inch apart on ungreased cookie sheets.

Bake in a 375° oven for 7 to 8 minutes or until the bottoms are lightly browned. Cool for 1 minute on cookie sheets. Transfer cookies to wire racks; cool completely. **Makes about 40 cookies.**

For each Santa: Reserve half of the icing. Color remaining icing with red coloring. For hat, use a paintbrush that is used only for food to paint top third of cookie with red icing. Place on wire rack and sprinkle with nonpareils. Let dry until set.

For beard, paint bottom half of cookie with reserved white icing. Sprinkle with coconut and let dry slightly. With a small dab of icing, attach candies for nose and eye. Let dry until set.

For each Elf: Reserve a little of the icing. Color remaining icing with green food coloring. For hat and suit, use a paintbrush that is used only for food to paint with green icing (see photo at *left*). Place on wire rack and sprinkle with green sugar. Let dry. For beard and hat trim, paint with reserved white icing. Sprinkle crystal sugar on hat trim. Let dry. With a small dab of icing, attach candies for nose, cheeks, and eyes. Let dry until set.

**Jingle Bell
Santa**

JINGLE BELL SANTAS

*Bell-shaped cookie cutters form these spicy
Santa cookies.*

1½ cups all-purpose flour

1 cup whole wheat flour

1 teaspoon baking soda

½ teaspoon ground cinnamon

¼ teaspoon salt

¼ teaspoon ground allspice

½ cup butter (no substitutes)

½ cup packed brown sugar

1 egg

⅓ cup honey

1 teaspoon vanilla

2 recipes Snow Frosting
(see recipe at *right*)
Paste food coloring, red
and/or green
Miniature chocolate pieces,
small decorating candies,
and rouge luster dust (optional)

Stir together all-purpose flour, whole
wheat flour, baking soda, cinnamon,
salt, and allspice in a medium bowl.

In a large mixing bowl, beat butter
with an electric mixer on medium to
high speed for 30 seconds or until
softened. Add brown sugar and beat
until fluffy. Beat in egg, honey, and
vanilla until combined. Beat in as
much of the flour mixture as you can
with the mixer. Stir in remaining
flour mixture with a wooden spoon.
Divide dough in half. Wrap in plastic
wrap. Chill 2 to 24 hours.

Roll half of the dough on a
lightly floured surface to ¼-inch
thickness. Cut into bell shapes with
a 2½- to 3-inch cookie cutter. Place
two inches apart on an ungreased
cookie sheet.

Bake in a 375° oven for 6 to 7
minutes or until edges are light
brown. Transfer cookies to wire
racks; cool completely. Repeat
with remaining dough.

Color some of the frosting with
red food coloring. If desired, color
some of the frosting with green
coloring. Leave remaining frosting
white. Fill pastry bags fitted with
small star tips or small round tips
with the white and colored frostings.

Pipe on hat, hat trim, and beard
as shown in photos. With small dabs
of frosting, attach chocolate pieces
and candies for eyes, nose, mouth,
and pom-pom on hat, if desired.
Let dry until set. Use luster dust for
cheeks, if desired.
Makes about 42 cookies.

SNOW FROSTING

*Ideal for piping on decorations, this
frosting is made with shortening rather
than butter for the truest colors.*

½ cup shortening

½ teaspoon vanilla

2⅓ cups sifted powdered sugar
Milk

Beat shortening and vanilla in a bowl
with an electric mixer on medium
speed for 30 seconds. Slowly add 1⅓
cups of the powdered sugar, beating
well. Add 1 tablespoon milk.

Gradually beat in remaining sugar
and enough milk (3 to 4 teaspoons)
to make a frosting of piping
consistency. **Makes about 1¼ cups.**

**Jingle Bell
Santas**

Gingerbread
Santa & Elf

GINGERBREAD SANTAS & ELVES

*Decorate these cookies with red suits for
Santas or green vests and whimsical
hats for Santa's elves.*

½   cup shortening
½   cup granulated sugar
1   teaspoon baking powder
1   teaspoon ground ginger
½   teaspoon baking soda
½   teaspoon ground cinnamon
½   teaspoon ground cloves
½   cup molasses
1   egg
1   tablespoon vinegar
2½ cups all-purpose flour
    Powdered Sugar Icing (see
       recipe, *page 157*)
    Paste food coloring, red
       and/or green
    Pearl sugar and small
    decorating candies

Beat shortening in a large mixing
bowl with an electric mixer on
medium to high speed for 30
seconds. Add sugar, baking powder,

ginger, baking soda, cinnamon,
and cloves. Beat until combined,
scraping sides of bowl occasionally.
Beat in molasses, egg, and vinegar.
Beat in as much of the flour as you
can with the mixer. Stir in remaining
flour with a wooden spoon. Divide
dough in half. Cover and chill for 3
hours or until easy to handle.

Grease a cookie sheet; set aside.
Roll half of the dough on a lightly
floured surface to ¼-inch thickness.
Cut into 3×1½-inch triangles. Place
1 inch apart on the prepared
cookie sheet. Slightly curve the top
of each triangle for tip of hat.

Bake in a 375° oven for 6 to 8
minutes or until edges are lightly
browned. Cool on cookie sheet for
1 minute. Transfer to wire racks;
cool completely. Repeat with
remaining dough.

Reserve about ¼ cup Powdered
Sugar Icing. Color the remaining
icing with red or green food
coloring. Use a paintbrush that is
used only for food or a knife to
paint or spread icing on cookies for
hat and Santa's suit or elf's vest,
leaving a plain area for the face.
Sprinkle with pearl sugar for the fur
trim. With small dabs of icing,
attach decorating candies for eyes,
nose, and buttons. Paint or pipe
beard or mustache with reserved
white icing. Let dry until set.

Santa-in-
the-Moon
Cookie

SANTA-IN-THE-MOON COOKIES

*Dress up a platter of plain cookies with a
few of these out-of-this-world Santas.*

Santa Cutouts dough (see recipe,
   ***page 154*)**
Egg Paint (see recipe at *right*)
Powdered Sugar Icing (see recipe,
   ***page 157*)**
Fine sanding sugar
Snow Frosting (see recipe,
   ***page 155*)**
Black paste food coloring
Small red cinnamon candies

Roll dough on a lightly floured
surface to ⅛-inch thickness. Cut
into crescent-moon shapes using a
2½-inch cookie cutter. Place 1 inch
apart on an ungreased cookie sheet.
Paint the hat area with Egg Paint as
shown in photo, *page 157*.

Bake in a 375° oven for 7 to 8
minutes or until the bottoms are
lightly browned. Cool 1 minute on
cookie sheet. Transfer to wire racks;
cool completely.

For each cookie, spread beard and hatband with Powdered Sugar Icing. Sprinkle with sanding sugar. Color 2 tablespoons of the Snow Frosting with black food coloring; set aside. Fill a pastry bag fitted with a medium star tip with white frosting. Pipe on mustache and pom-pom on hat.

With a dab of frosting, attach a red candy for the nose. Fill pastry bag fitted with a small star tip with black frosting. Pipe on a tiny star for the eye. Let dry until set. **Makes about 45 cookies.**

Egg Paint: Stir together 1 *egg yolk* and 2 drops *water.* Stir in *red paste food coloring* to make desired shade.

Jolly Santa

JOLLY SANTAS
So simple, so cheerful—turn an ordinary triangle into a jolly old Santa.

    Santa Cutouts dough (see recipe, *page 154*)
    Powdered Sugar Icing (see recipe *at right*)
    Paste food coloring, red and black
    Snow Frosting (see recipe, *page 155*)

Roll dough on a lightly floured surface to ⅛-inch thickness. Cut into triangles with 3-inch sides. Place 1 inch apart on an ungreased cookie sheet. Bake in a 375° oven for 7 to 8 minutes or until the bottoms are lightly browned. Cool 1 minute on cookie sheet. Transfer to wire racks and cool completely.

Color Powdered Sugar Icing with red food coloring. Decorate each triangle with red icing as shown in the photo at *right.* Let dry until set.

Color 2 tablespoons of the Snow Frosting with black food coloring; set aside. Fill a pastry bag fitted with a medium star tip with white frosting. Pipe on beard, hatband, pom-pom on hat, and belt buckle.

Fill a pastry bag fitted with a writing tip with black frosting. Pipe on belt and eye. Let dry until set. **Makes about 40 cookies.**

POWDERED SUGAR ICING
Light cream or half-and-half gives this icing the shiniest look.

    4   cups sifted powdered sugar
    1   teaspoon vanilla
    3   to 4 tablespoons half-and-half, light cream, or milk

Combine powdered sugar, vanilla, and cream or milk. Stir in additional cream or milk, 1 teaspoon at a time, until icing is easy to drizzle. **Makes about 2 cups.**

DECORATING TIPS
- Let cookies cool completely on wire racks before frosting. Allow about 15 minutes.
- Paste food coloring offers a wide range of colors, gives intense color, and doesn't thin the frosting.
- For simple designs, substitute a heavy self-sealing plastic bag for a pastry bag. Spoon the icing into the bag and snip off one corner. A small hole will produce a fine line or tiny dollop; a larger hole makes a wider line or bigger dollop.
- Make sure the frosting is thick enough to hold the piping shape but still thin enough to squeeze easily from the bag.

■ ■ ■

Santa-in-the-Moon Cookies

Use a small paintbrush to brush Egg Paint onto Santa-in-the-Moon Cookies before baking. The oven's heat will set the paint.

Jolly Santas

Use a pastry bag fitted with a writing tip to outline the area for the red suit for Jolly Santas. Pipe squiggles of red icing onto the area. Smooth the icing with a thin spatula.

Sources

Lasting Legends

A Man on a Mission, *pages 10–15*
Sergeant Santa, Inc., 3023 West Marshall Street,
P.O. Box 6665, Richmond, VA 23230;
804/358-7281.

A Midwest Father Christmas, *pages 16–21*
For more information on Father Christmas and
his troupe, contact Alan Lance Andersen, Theatre
of Interactive Drama, Inc., 122 West Ash Lane,
Roland, IA 50236; e-mail: andersen@iastate.edu;
515/388-5573.

Timeless Memorabilia

Sweet (Santa) Success, *pages 28–33*
Vaillancourt Folk Art, 145 Armsby Road, Sutton,
MA 01590; 877/665-2244; e-mail: valfa@valfa.com;
www.vaillancourtfolkart.com.

Reviving an Old World Tradition, *pages 34–39*
D. Blümchen & Company, Inc.,
162 East Ridgewood Avenue, Ridgewood, NJ 07450;
201/652-5595; e-mail: dblumchenandco@aol.com;
www.blumchen.com.

Devoted Collectors

A Kris Kringle Colony, *pages 42–47*
Reasons to Believe, 92 Kirkland Avenue,
Kirkland, WA 98033; 877/893-8159;
www.reasonstobelieve.com.

Master Crafters

Unveiling Beauty, *pages 70–75*
Spindlenicks, Bradley Bruinsma, P.O. Box 5731,
Lafayette, IN 47903.

Front Porch Santas, *pages 76–83*
Creations by Jan, 219 South 8th Street,
Opelika, AL 36801; 334/741-7040.

In the Nick of Time, *pages 84–89*
Prairie Art Originals, 15525 Float Lane,
Apple Valley, MN 55124; 952/431-3523.

Woolly Wonders, *pages 90–95*
Woolsworth, 1000 Capitola Drive, Napa, CA 94559;
707/224-4034; www.woolsworth.net.

Honest Pots, *pages 96–101*
Monroe Salt Works, 76 Bartlett Hill Road,
Monroe, ME 04951; 888/525-4471.

Ally of the Dolls, *pages 102–109*
Old World Santas, 22910 Estoril #6, Diamond Bar,
CA 91765; 909/860-8007; e-mail: owsantas@aol.com.

Chain Saw Carver, *pages 110–115*
Corn Valley Carvings, 3234 Pioneer Drive SE,
Salem, OR 97302; 503/363-3464, e-mail:
woodsanta@hotmail.com.

Familiar Faces, *pages 116–121*
Original Art Sculptures, 4595 S. Park Hill Avenue,
Springfield, MO 65810; 417/883-4177; e-mail:
VanNoy-Art@msn.com.

*Many of the materials and items used in this book
are available at crafts and art supply stores. For more
information, please write or call the manufacturers listed.*

Personal Expressions

Hooked on Santa, *pages 124–127*
Wool and rug hook—Dorr Mill Store,
800/846-DORR.

Cotton Batting Santas, *pages 128–132*
All numbered items—D. Blümchen & Company, Inc.;
201/652-5595; www.blumchen.com.

Santa Ornament Trio, *pages 133–137*
Caron Kit Kin thread—The Caron Collection,
203/381-9999; www.caron-net.com.

Mill Hill seed and bugle beads—Mill Hill;
www.millhillbeads.com; e-mail: millhill@millhill.com.

Kreinik Blending Filament and Gold Braid—Kreinik
Mfg. Co., Inc; 800/537-2166; www.kreinik.com.

Elegant Father Christmas Doll, *pages 138–141*
Porcelain Doll parts (Old-fashioned Santa head
with hands 1231-28)—Darice, 800/321-1494;
www.darice.com.

Sign of the Times, *pages 142–145*
Delta Ceramcoat acrylic paint—Delta Technical
Coatings, Inc.; 800/423-4135; www.deltacrafts.com.

Saral Transfer Paper—Saral Paper Corp.;
212/223-3322; www.saralpaper.com.

Innkeeper Sign (14071W)—Walnut Hollow;
800/950-5101; www.walnuthollow.com.

Cross-Stitch Stand-Up Santas, *pages 146–149*
Parchment Aida cloth—Wichelt Imports, Inc.,
www.wichelt.com.

Sweet Sensations

Sweet Santas, *pages 152-157*
Mini Star Cake Pan—Wilton Industries;
800/794-5866; www.wilton.com.

COLLECTION

Creative Director: Patricia Church Podlasek

Executive Editor: Mary L. Heaton
Project Editors: Dave Kirchner, Veronica Koh
Associate Art Director: Carrie Topp
Photo Stylists: Patty Crawford, Cherie Dale
Administrative Assistant: Cathy Celsi
Contributing Copy Editor: Babs Klein
Contributing Writer: Lisa Sloan

Contributing Graphic Designer: Heather Hardt
Contributing Illustrators: Glenda Aldrich, Barbara Gordon,
Chris Neubauer Graphics

Vice President, Publishing Director
William R. Reed

Publisher: Maureen Ruth
Consumer Product Marketing Director: Ben Jones
Consumer Product Marketing Manager: Karrie Nelson
Business Manager: Jie Lin
Production Manager: Douglas M. Johnston
Book Production Managers: Pam Kvitne, Marjorie J. Schenkelberg
Assistant to the Publisher: Cheryl Eckert

Meredith Publishing Group
Publishing Group President: Stephen M. Lacy
President, Magazine Group: Jerry Kaplan
Corporate Solutions: Michael Brownstein
Creative Services: Ellen de Lathouder
Manufacturing: Bruce Heston
Consumer Marketing: Karla Jeffries
Finance: Max Runciman

CORPORATION
Chairman and CEO: William T. Kerr
Chairman of the Executive Committee: E.T. Meredith III

Member

For editorial questions, please write:
Better Homes and Gardens® Santa Claus Collection, Vol. 4
1716 Locust St., GA 202, Des Moines, IA 50309-3023

ISSN: 1524-9794   ISBN: 0-696-21515-2

Believe!